LISTENING TO SPIRIT:
ONE LIGHTWORKER'S STORY

LISTENING TO SPIRIT: ONE LIGHTWORKER'S STORY

Channelings and Stories from the Life of Joseph Anthony

Copyright © 2024 Joseph Anthony

All rights reserved. If you copy or quote parts of this book, please cite the source. Thank you for respecting the work that has gone into this book.

CONTACT: JosephAnthony@ListeningtoSpirit.net

ISBN 978-0-9965103-9-4

eISBN 979-8-9909292-0-3

LIBRARY OF CONGRESS CONTROL NUMBER: 2024913217

Cover design by Robin Locke Monda

Interior design by Phillip Gessert

Set in Garamond

Cover image used under license from istockphoto.com

Author photo by Laura B.

Dedication

I dedicate this book to the manifestation of Spirit that I hold most dear, my wife Laura, who has been my loving companion during many lifetimes.

TABLE OF CONTENTS

Introduction xi

PART 1: ATTUNEMENTS AND INFORMATION PROVIDED THROUGH CHANNELED SESSIONS 1

How to read this section 3

Personal Guides and an Early Channeling: 11-6-08 5

The Changing Energy Is Pushing Up More of the True Self: 9-23-09 9

Guidance for the Healing Light Group: 7-12-12 11

We Are Ancient Beings of Knowledge: 7-20-14 15

Connecting to the Universal Vibrational Level: 8-14-14 19

Light, Purity, and Connection: 12-13-14 21

The Sounds of Heaven Are All Around Us: 8-22-15 25

We Are an Encapsulated Piece of Source: 10-24-15 27

We Volunteered for this Existence from Higher Dimensional Levels: 3-12-16 29

An Energy Activation: 2016 31

Accept that We Are Who We Are: 3-8-17 35

The Old Negative System Is Crumbling: 6-8-17 37

A Transformative Cosmic Energy Wave is Coming: 6-8-17 39

We Are All One Being: 6-8-17 41

A Heart Connection to the Source: 10-28-17 43

Three Dragons: 1-22-18 47

Step Up from the Words of Loving All to Being the Love of All: 1-25-18 49

The Light Is the Same in All of Us: 3-10-18 53

Expanding to the Size of the Sun: 6-27-18 57

Working Together: 6-30-18 59

We Cannot Minimize Who We Are: 6-30-18 61

Become One with the Earth: 7-13-18 63

Our Soul Is Our Guide: 7-13-18 67

Dragons are the Seraphim: 12-4-18 69

We Are a Platoon of Lightworkers: 12-8-2018 71

The Power of the Heart Consciousness Is Immense: 1-26-19 73

The Nature of the Soul: 1-29-19 77

An Example of the Energy of Crystals: 4-4-19 83

You Have to Feed the Dragons Every Day: 4-13-19 87

The Role of the Lightworkers: 4-23-19 89

We are the World: 4-27-19 93

The Energy of Release: 6-26-19 95

Effort is Not Needed: 7-6-19 99

Ask for Assistance: 9-3-19 101

Medieval Times and a Dragon Companion: 3-4-20 103

Working with the Transition: 3-4-20 105

Recycling the Energy of Pain and Fear: 8-11-21 107

Higher Level Energy: 8-11-21 109

There Is Only One Kind of Healing: 8-11-21 115

The Vibration of Creation: 8-11-21 117

PART 2: LIVING IN THE LIGHT 121
About this Section 123

Strong Intuition Prevents Possible Paralysis: October, 1978 125
Saved with a Roll of Paper Towels: March, 1989 127
Forty-to-One Odds Against Getting in to Graduate School: 1994 129
Hummingbirds: 8-25-11 and 8-28-18 133
Rooster Comb Mountain: October, 2014 135
Topaz: July, 2023 141

PART 3: CLOSING THOUGHTS 143
With Love and Light 145

Notes 151
Acknowledgements 153
About the Author 155

INTRODUCTION

THE ONLY THING you really need to know is that all is God and all is good. For those of you who understand this, there is no need to read any further. This book is for those who are seeking greater understanding about the nature of God at work in our world and, in a very personal way, in our lives. I draw from my own life experiences for illustrations, which have revealed the omnipresence of God, the nature of the soul, the work of Lightworkers, and the guidance available from ethereal spirits such as angels, dragons and departed masters. I also include some examples from my own life about the flow of life when attuned to a fourth dimensional consciousness.

My spiritual unfolding began in my early twenties with a profound experience of cosmic unity. I was walking on a mountain road at the time and the entire world suddenly shifted. I saw everything as a single divine, loving, conscious energy. Nothing was excluded; even the air was conscious and appeared as dancing pinpoints of light. I knew instantly this was a direct experience of God, although it was not like any aspect of God ever explained to me in the church. This was the true reality, and what I had previously thought to be real was, as one of my later teachers said, only a "play of consciousness."

Prior to this experience, I was not religious, having abandoned the Catholicism of my parents when I was a teenager. I was, however, actively searching for and pondering the meaning and purpose of life. While I had no particular beliefs regarding the nature or even the existence of God, I was open to new understandings regarding spirituality.

Although my experience of cosmic unity lasted under a minute, it has been the defining event in my life; and nearly fifty years later is still the guiding force behind my beliefs and actions. The experience opened up an active channel to the higher realms for me that manifests in my life as enhanced intuition and occasional direct messages and guidance from higher beings. Also, the understanding that all is God has shaped my beliefs about everything.

Fortunately, one of the first people I told about my experience encouraged me to explore Eastern religions where mystical events like mine have been described by many teachers. This initial exploration led me to read broadly about religions, both Eastern and Western, as well as to visit an ashram in the Catskills where I learned to meditate and gained appreciation for the value of repeating a mantra. While at a retreat at this ashram, I had my second profound mystical experience. It occurred during a 24-hour chant of the usually silent mantra "Om Namah Shivaya." Sometime during the middle of the night, after many hours of chanting, everything around me disappeared, and I both saw and experienced Om Namah Shivaya as an unimaginably powerful cosmic vibration. It emerged from emptiness and rolled across my field of vision like a great wave leaving our fully formed universe in its wake. This experience left my mind and my understanding of the universe greatly expanded. It was also clear to me that many before me must have had similar experiences; both the understanding that all is God and the use of Om Namah Shivaya as a mantra are widespread.

Subsequent experiences in the form of vivid dreams and visions during meditation led me to understand that I had lived multiple times; that my death would be a joyous homecoming with those I had previously loved as well as with a host of spiritual beings; that time is merely an artificial construct and that all events actually occur simultaneously in the mind of God; that this earthly existence is a school to learn to become more loving and to use power responsibly; and that we have divine guidance available to us at all times.

While my new spiritual experiences and understandings were wonderful, they did not afford me any immunity from life's problems and difficulties. But they did provide great peace of mind, which was then always available to me. This turned out to be incredibly valuable when I was diagnosed with stage III Hodgkin's disease at age twenty-five, just ten weeks after getting married. My treatment for that cancer was very difficult, including ninety-two radiation treatments, a major surgery, and several very painful medical procedures. Unfortunately, that was not the end of it. I had many very troublesome health problems over that next decade including a recurrence and progression of my cancer to stage IV resulting in an additional major surgery to my right lung and twelve rounds of very debilitating chemotherapy.

One thing that really helped me during my years of illness, especially during chemotherapy, were my frequent sessions with a polarity therapist. Judy was a wonderful healer, and I found her energy treatments to be sustaining. Several years after the completion of my chemotherapy, Judy introduced me to her friend Sage, an energy healer and medical intuitive who channeled angelic messages. Her ability to channel was truly astounding. I had many healing/channeling sessions with Sage, most of which I recorded. This book is a compilation of many of those sessions along with messages I have been blessed to receive from other gifted channelers, often during healing energy treatments.

In 2012, I was guided along with Johanna, Sage and Judy, who appear throughout the book as healers and channelers, to set up a healing group, which became known as the Healing Light Group. It was composed of sixteen Lightworkers/healers who met twice monthly for two hours for approximately seven years. We generally saw two clients at each session on a pro bono basis. We worked together as a group to provide energy treatments, which included channeling and utilized crystals and healing meditation. These were intended to address not only the specific needs or problems of the person, but also such problems throughout the world. Some of the transcribed channeled sessions that follow are from those meetings.

I had to learn, as I was increasingly drawn into this spiritual realm, that it is often not understood by others who have not had such a personal experience. I was hesitant to talk about my experiences because I might be considered delusional or weird. I felt uncomfortable talking about them to anyone other than my wife and the few people I knew who worked with energy healing. Until a decade ago, I had no intention of ever sharing this information more broadly and am doing so now only because I was encouraged to do so during three different channeling sessions. I came to understand that reading about my experiences would help others to believe that their own metaphysical experiences, however unusual, are valid. I was also told that some of the information I had received needed to be more widely disseminated.

This book is a compilation of some of my spiritual experiences and learnings, offered in the hope that others might find them useful. It is divided into two main sections followed by my closing thoughts and a few notes on terms that may be unfamiliar. Section one is the transcriptions of channelings that I recorded over a thirteen-year period. I have pulled a phrase from the channeling itself to use as a descriptor for the table of contents. Section two of this book has examples of the visible presence of divine guidance/intervention in my life. These two sections might be thought of as the metaphysical and day-to-day or practical components of life, respectively. I see them as intertwined.

My adult journey started when I was a young man seeking to

find the purpose of life. As I described earlier, that search resolved in a profound way. Since then, my life work has been learning to put into daily practice the knowledge that all is God. I hope that the words I have put down on paper can help others on their spiritual paths by pointing out markers, describing interesting features, telling a few stories, and sharing some of the knowledge from my own journey.

>With love and light,
>JOSEPH ANTHONY

PART 1:

ATTUNEMENTS AND INFORMATION PROVIDED THROUGH CHANNELED SESSIONS

PART I

HOW TO READ THIS SECTION

THE CHANNELING SESSIONS in this section are in chronological order, and I have been as faithful to the recordings as possible in each transcription, making changes largely for brevity, to enhance clarity and for readability. The channelings often involved connecting with spiritual beings and always contained information and understandings that were new to us and were often profound. In addition, the sessions were almost always energetic events that cleared energy blockages and patterns that were no longer necessary and attuned us to increasingly higher vibrational frequencies. I say us because the channeler and I typically took the same energetic journey, which we would then share with our healing group. We were often left woozy or light-headed, and it would be an understatement to say it was not always clear what we were supposed to do with the new insights or how we were supposed to make the changes that were at times indicated. It sometimes took us months or longer to fully integrate and adjust to what occurred in these sessions.

Looking back, I see these sessions as way-stops on a spiritual journey that I traveled with my close companions and healing group members that was always leading to greater understanding and deeper connection to divinity, a journey of discovery of the true self that continues to this moment. It is my hope that, where appropriate, some of the energetic information we experienced will be conveyed to the reader. If so, it will probably take time.

PERSONAL GUIDES
AND AN EARLY CHANNELING

Sage, 11-6-08

*S*AGE BEGINS BY *passing on comments from her spirit guide during a healing session for Joe.*

SAGE: Everything has energy. This large amethyst crystal under the massage table is setting up a field because there is going to be vibrational work. He is telling me that he will set up the energy to allow a master vibration to come in. Now he is showing me a Chinese Mandarin Scholar in a very old style orange robe who looks like he is from an ancient monastery. His hair is in a long braid down his back, he has a long thin mustache, and his hands are holding his forearms. He is called the Wise One.

He says, "I am a master of many sorts, and I have been with you before. It is time that we reconnect. Know that you have the power to be a channel of change because of how you vibrate, how you look at the world, and your belief that the world can right itself. So know that as with many others, you are part of the change. You will be given information and guided to receive what you need to receive." He is a very strong individual and he tells me he is one of your teachers now. You have to give him permission to work with you if that is what you want.

JOE: Is he a being I should trust?

SAGE: Yes, but he say always check intuitively because there are others who are similar but not the same. He was a scholar who spent his life studying. I do not even think he even came outside the monastery. He just studied there all his life and meditated. Whenever you want to communicate, set your intent that it will be for the highest and best purpose of creation. There is something about a female coming in to work with you also. She is Native American and provides the gentle balance. They are blending their cultures and their wisdom to communicate with you. They said that even if you were not aware, you have received whispers. You need to know that your judgments are solid and have no doubt about that.

Did you work today?

JOE: Yes.

SAGE: When you go to the hospital, surround yourself in an energy field or screen which allows that which is necessary to come to you and releases that which is not for your highest good. He wants to know if you know that you are a healer.

JOE: Yes.

SAGE: Ok. Then you know that there are people who work around you that need healing. He said all you have to do is nonverbally send healing energy to them. You can simply send it; it is their choice to accept it or not. Always have a clear intent and always let it be their choice. When we want them to do something specific, we muddy the waters. The energy flows more freely when our clear intent is for their highest and best purpose.

JOE: My intent can just be for their highest and best for them? I don't have to be specific?

SAGE: Yes. It's not necessary for us to make any decisions about what is needed.

Sage: He says many people are going be vehicles to bring in light on a higher vibrational level into this world. People will begin to notice and be drawn to that light. One of the things happening now is that the earth is supporting negativity less and less. People that are negative are having increasing problems, because energetically, the earth is pushing them to look at things in a much more positive way.

The Wise One says that you are a spiritual man and have a spiritual light. That is a gift but it also can become overwhelming. He said that when you are given such a gift, you will be guided to be and do and go where you need to. He is saying that there are no coincidences, and then he said it again to make sure that you really hear his message. He said throughout your life, they will manipulate things so that what you need is always there.

THE CHANGING ENERGY IS PUSHING UP MORE OF THE TRUE SELF

Sage, 9-23-09

SAGE BEGINS BY passing on comments from her spirit guide during a healing session for Joe.

SAGE: He said people are going to be opened up to a more truly natural way of being. The way we have been living is more of a falsehood of our true self. It has been: I have to get an education; I have to have two cars, etc. It has been more of a focus on the material aspects of life. The changing energy of the Earth is pushing up more of the true self and more and more people are going to respond to that energy. Some people who do not want to shift might get very uncomfortable or even have a breakdown before they do because they can't stop their negative energy.

What is happening on the Earth right now is actually a very good thing because it is cleansing. The more people who wake up to what their true being is, the more the energy of peace can come to Earth. They are showing me that only when you are in that peaceful space can you bring that energy of true peace in and radiate that peace. Instead of the mental and verbal, "I want peace on earth," it is about being it and feeling the essence of it. This is what changes the vibratory energy of discord between peoples.

They just took me up in your spiritual fields and I saw a shift happening. A high vibratory energy, almost like high knowledge, is coming into your spiritual field. This is not learning knowledge, it is feeling and vibrational knowledge.

He said this isn't the greatest analogy but think of being a person in a Catholic Church and the person next to you is the Dali Lama. Not that either one is good or bad, but they are at totally different vibrational levels. Because here you are just a practicing Catholic, here you have integrated love into your body so much you radiate it unconsciously.

GUIDANCE FOR THE HEALING LIGHT GROUP

Sage and Judy, 7-12-12

THIS HEALING SESSION *for Joe began with a long channeling by Sage from three beings self-identified as Light, Lighter, and Lightest from the middle star in the Belt of Orion.*

SAGE: You have gathered like souls around you because they support your work in this world. It is our pleasure to assist you and them. You are special beings that bring a vibration into this Earth that not all can carry. It helps with the transition (see the Notes Section) and increases vibrations worldwide. You are in a place and time of fear and uncertainty of what will be and how it will be. Know that all is in order and when you have even a small amount of fear, you resist the vibrations. So monitor yourself and ask us to assist you in releasing fear. Your heart is pure and it vibrates in sync with those in your core group. Be aware that you all need to work at the heart level, so connect energetically with each person's heart for a few moments each time you meet.

As you know, you are healers of high magnitude. You know some of those places that you have been before. Some of those with you have also been there. That is where you learned some of your healing skills. You must be open to more knowledge of healing to come to you and into you. It will come from this star, and it will not be what you know now. You must all release your resistance and be open to that occurring.

We support your world and we support your mission. When you ask, we will assist. Our mission is to hold you all in the light and to hold you in the space that you need to be in to be excellent receivers. As you know, you are a catalyst and you open the receiving first. Do not fear anything because we understand the sacred beings that you are far better than you. We understand your humanness and will assist you through whatever you need. But you must ask us when you want that.

There is a reason the Pyramids in Egypt were aligned with the three stars in the Belt of Orion. The ancient beings knew of the energies within that constellation. They knew things were aligned for the energies to be able to be worked with here on the Earth plane. They are coded with the ancient information, some of which will be downloaded to you and others to assist on this planet. There was also an energetic alignment from the tip of the pyramid to the stars that held a vibration that people in the current timeframe and forward will need to assist with bringing peace into your world.

We have to ask all of you to work on doubt. That is currently one of the most destructive energies to our assisting in this world. Doubt is like putting up the Great Wall of China as a barrier to change for the greater good. So if we ask you to do anything, we ask everyone to work on removing doubt about what you can do and who you are. Ask for doubt to be taken from you and ask that you may be in the flow, because from there you can hold the vibration that is needed for yourself, for peace, and for unconditional acceptance of all beings.

Next is a conversation immediately following the healing energy session that Sage and Judy gave Joe. It refers to the one-finger light touch healing technique that Sage and Judy were instructed to use.

JOE: This session was not just for me; it was a message to our group. We have work to do.

JUDY: We must verbalize our requests for help.

JOE: We also must connect at the heart level before we begin our work.

SAGE: He said the reason we had to work with one finger was a matter of trust, because we need to reach the level of trust where we can touch and know that whatever is supposed to be will be.

JOE: So the work is effortless when you are in the right spot. Touch and it happens.

SAGE: Yes, yes. You can do all the other stuff, and sometimes that is necessary. But it is exactly as you said: when you are in that spot, a touch and it will be done.

JOE: That is what Jesus did: he did not do a half hour of bodywork on somebody. He just touched them.

JUDY: Believe and it shall be.

SAGE: It will be difficult because we are taught that we cannot do as Jesus did.

JOE: We have to unlearn that.

SAGE: Yes, exactly, and he is telling me that the unlearning that is an important concept for the group. He says there are some who will struggle.

JOE: Who won't?

ALL: (Laughter)

WE ARE ANCIENT BEINGS OF KNOWLEDGE

Sage, 7-20-14

SAGE BEGINS BY *passing on comments from her spirit guide during a healing session for Joe.*

SAGE: I am picking up the presence of Spirit Guardians, that is different they said than spirit guides or spirit beings. The ancient ones are here and also star seeds, star beings, angelic beings, and both the Arcturians (See the Notes Section) and another group from the Belt of Orion. That latter unnamed group is the one currently giving you an energetic infusion. They just showed me there has been a connection between us in many lifetimes going back to Atlantis. You were a scientist secretly working to counteract negative things that others were doing. You worked with crystals and knew how to make them work together in a way that could greatly magnify their potential. It is why you have such an affinity for crystals now. They are showing me that you were my uncle, and I used to play with and talk to the crystals.

You knew the cycle of what was happening, and you knew that at some later point, all of those from there would meet again, as is currently happening. You are approaching a time when you will begin to communicate with these beings and many others; they have lined up and wait at this time. They say to tell you that you are a teacher, and the time to be that is drawing closer.

THE SPIRIT GUARDIAN SPEAKING THROUGH SAGE: We from Orion are teaching you healing, and we are going to include knowledge and communication on levels you are not aware of. We will eventually introduce you to a spiritual knowing on a level above where you are now. You need to practice asking questions and looking quickly for the answer, knowing that it will be there. It is like 1, 2, 3; 1) question, 2) know the answer will be there, and 3) answer. Just 1, 2, 3; it will be that fast because that is the process that we use. We understand that in your world things are different, and this is not how you normally work. You have been chosen again to be this, to be a leader, a teacher, and a guide for others. And this must expand beyond one receiver.

We come from far away from your world, and we are the seeds in which the stars come from. We bring the light into your world through individuals. We ask you to bring that light of those stars into your group as they are ready; you will know how to do this. It needs to be initiated with a touch to the crown or the heart, and they must be asked to expand this. We are ancient beings of knowledge, and we are proud to be asked to come and work in your world. We have much to give, and you and others are able to receive our communications. We come from many cultures and are what you might call the "Grand Mothers." We at one time resided in your world and went through many lifetimes in which we gained a great understanding of how your world works, so that we can share with you and others in a way that will work within your world. It is a precious world, a place of light and a place where love is growing greatly. You been activated by many things, and it is time to blend those things which you do not have words for, and then ground it into your being.

JOE: The work is different now; it is just infusions of frequencies of light at levels I do not understand.

SAGE: This is being done at more than one level, and at the same time they are giving me an infusion. He said we have our physical world, our spiritual world, and then we have our entire universe. You can think of it as an infusion of light, information and communication from all three.

Spirit talking through Sage: Because you are working as a group, it is important that the group knows that it is ready to achieve and communicate at a different level. It is possible, whether it is believed or not. You are to ask them to infuse into their being the light of change, the light of true knowledge of who they are beyond their humanness, and for them to know that they are exactly where they are supposed to be. No one is there by accident, and no one is at a different level than others. Some are communicators of information and light, but all have the same gifts if they choose to use them. So we again tell you to tell them that they are blessed, and have been chosen to do this work. For that, we thank them greatly because they can be vehicles which manifest our work in your world.

Joe: I am honored by their presence and allowing us to contribute to this.

Sage: They are unique and sacred beings, and they truly appreciate our allowing them to work through us. We have been chosen because we can step aside for them to do their work.

Joe: It sounds so simple. Just say yes; let them do it, and try not to get in the way.

Sage: That is the hard part.

CONNECTING TO THE UNIVERSAL VIBRATIONAL LEVEL

Dinner Gathering of Five Healing Light Group Members, 8-14-14

T*HE DISCUSSION AND channeling below is related to a message to Joe about connecting to a higher vibrational energy.*

JOE: This is about connecting to the universal vibrational level. If you think of the physical level we live at, and then the spiritual level to which we have been connecting to all along, this is a jump up from that to what they are calling the universal level. We've had some experience with universal beings from that level, so it is not like we haven't had some contact there in the past. They said that we can refer to them as the Grand Mothers. They want to work with our group and said we are now ready. I believe that's the level they wanted us to get to all along. I don't know that there will be a level beyond this that we are going to be working at. We now have been refined enough because of the work that has been done on us that we can connect, hold the space, and channel the energies for them.

JOHANNA: They keep telling us to get out of the way.

JOE: Yes, that was absolutely clear. Connect and let them do the work, and do your best to not interfere.

SAGE: We are not doing work anymore; it will be totally them, and there will be work at both the physical and the universal levels. I am seeing that an object in the shape of a triangular shaft will be the embodiment of this connection. They are telling me that we need to build it in order to experience the effect it will have.

Joe: This will be an enormous conduit of energy. Just like a fluorescent lightbulb needs to have an electrical connection at each end for the electricity to flow, the energy from the universal level needs a connection here for the flow to occur. We are the lower connection point and the universal beings are the upper one. The flow mostly comes from them down, but we have to be here to complete the circuit.

Sage: We have to send energy and light up to them to keep the communication going. They said it is not just about communication because in order for them to work through us, they have to know us, and this communication helps them to know us.

Joe: Part of that communication is sharing with them our own vibrational frequencies as humans and the vibrational frequencies of the clients we work on. That helps them know what energy is most useful. They are so far removed from us; they have trouble distinguishing what are the specific wavelengths of our disharmonious vibrational patterns, and we act as a kind of scout for them saying this is the pattern.

Johanna: They need us to help translate energy as well. Their energy comes through very high, and if we are working on somebody else, they may need to tone it down by sending it through us so we can step it down to a lower frequency before passing it on to someone.

LIGHT, PURITY, AND CONNECTION

The Healing Light Group, 12-13-14

JOE SHOWS THE *Healing Light Group* the triangular prism (referred to later as a pillar) that he purchased to represent the energetic connection that was talked about on 8-14-14 at his house.

❖

JOE: My thought is that this prism can represent the connection between us and the beings at the universal level.

SAGE: It really brings in a lot of depth and a lot of emotion. It is a pillar that brings through the strength, the grace and the core through which they can work. Because it is pure, it comes uninterrupted, and we need to be pure and uninterrupted in our connection. To do that, we need to feel the energy go up from our solar plexus and allow them to connect. They will then do what is necessary to make the connection. Once they do that, it is a pure complete connection to energy and healing beyond what we can even understand.

The three sides and the shape provide balance, and also bring the energy form all cultures, from Egyptian to Native American to those we don't even know about because they have not yet been found on earth. All of that is brought forth. The pillar has a core of light, through which we will be able to work. They are sending an incredible amount of blessings for the work that we are willing to do.

SAGE: One side is purity, one side is light, and one side is them and the connection to them. This is a point beyond where we have normally gone. They are asking that when we are ready to connect, that we be pure in our intention and feel the energy within moving up so that they can make the connection. It is extremely high magnitude energy, and we have all asked to work with it before. They keep using the word purity. He just said this is a gift we're giving you because working with this is so beyond what you can even know. The magnitude of what is happening is like a mushroom cloud of energy that's exploding around the world, and the more we connect with that energy, the more it can work.

He is saying that there is a fracture of energy that was created by negativity. This is the reason they're stepping things up now, because this energy has power and the strength to heal that fracture. The fracture will start to heal if we are willing to do our best with the components of those three sides. He said that is all it takes; just start working with it, and then they can do the rest. We can access this at any time. We just have to think of the components of purity, light and connection.

J.M.: To be clear, how do we work with this?

SAGE: That pillar is a representation. (Sage pointing to the three sides) This is purity; this is light, and this is them. So you go to purity… and what he is telling me is you have to try and feel this in your body. This is not passive; he wants us to be able with our energy to make a connection. So purity, light and our energy go up to them. They are showing me the universe and a flood of energy coming down, and that is what we are connecting to.

The next section occurred following a brief meditation during which we connected to this energy.

J.M.: It feels like a forgiving energy; forgiveness beyond what we even know.

SAGE: Yes.

JOHANNA: This is working on the negativity that has caused the communal helpless-hopeless feelings. It will bring people back into an area where they feel they can make a difference and give more value to each person.

SAGE: It is a very peaceful and loving energy. He said take any word you can think of; it is even beyond that. He said one word to use is encompassing; it just encompasses and changes.

DAN: It seems to me, whichever way you feel energy, that is the way it will come in. To me, it is just flooding my heart.

D.L.: I feel like my whole chest and my heart are just vibrating.

SAGE: To make this connection, there has to be involvement within you. If you can feel energy move up from your solar plexus, that makes a connection. He said all you need to do is think it, because it will happen. Once this starts, they direct it around the Earth and the universe as needed. They are already healing the fractured energy they showed me earlier. He said this is no longer in your hands.

D.L.: I am getting different visuals for purity. The first is a newborn baby and the second is a lotus flower.

SAGE'S SPIRIT GUIDE SPEAKING THROUGH SAGE: This is a way of transforming yourselves and the energies that you have worked with in the past. Know that purity is part of that for the magnificent reason that when things are pure, they can utilize all the higher vibrations. That will help you to make the changes that need to be made. I have assisted you in coming to this place, and I will continue to work with you. Many things can be changed as this new work starts, and know that it is an incredible blessing for you. As you live your life, recognize that you can choose to emanate that energy to anyone who passes by. You have to do nothing other than make that choice, so share the light.

THE SOUNDS OF HEAVEN ARE ALL AROUND US

The Healing Light Group, 8-22-15

JOE: SPIRIT asked me to mention a piece that clarified for me in my meditation this morning related to releasing the drama of life. It involved using a meditation technique I was taught to visualize climbing above my mind until I had no more thoughts, and to just climb higher every time my awareness went to a thought instead of to my mantra. I did that and went upward until I had no more thoughts and was able to experience completeness without thoughts. It was heavenly and very profound. Spirit later told me that all thoughts, including those about work, relationships, and grievances are at the third dimensional level. That's where the drama occurs; it is in our thoughts. So the guidance I received wasn't to change my thoughts to be more positive, or change my thoughts to be more loving, it was to transcend beyond thoughts. Then there's no drama; you are just experiencing whatever is there.

In an earlier meditation using this technique while listening to music, I was able to experience the music without thoughts, and I understood at a very deep level that I was experiencing the vibrational frequencies of heaven. Since then, I have used that technique many times to transcend my thoughts and simply be aware of what I was experiencing. It always turns out to be a vibrational frequency of heaven; not always beautiful music unless I happened to have that playing, but always the experience of heaven. So what I had was a deep experiential understanding that I actually live in heaven, and the sounds of heaven are all around me. It is unnecessary thoughts that distract me that keep me from experiencing peace as an ongoing reality.

L.P.: Is it safe to say that we are trying to lift out of the third dimensional drama, and that we would then be living our lives in the fourth dimension? What is the fourth dimension?

JOE: I think it's the same as the third physically. You don't change your body, you don't change your house, you still go to work, but your understanding is that this is an aspect of heaven. We are all heavenly creatures that are choosing to experience third dimensional reality for a while. Ideally, we do it with an understanding that this is heaven and to not get caught in the drama. It is like you are an actor playing the role of Hamlet. Remember you're playing the role of Hamlet, you're not really him. So if you have to act on stage like you are angry, that's fine, but when you get off stage, don't carry that anger. You have to let that go. Don't get caught in your role. In a similar fashion, when we link together and send healing energy worldwide, what we really are sending is the energy of release from the third dimensional drama.

WE ARE AN ENCAPSULATED PIECE OF SOURCE

The Healing Light Group, 10-24-15

JOE: THERE is a piece that came to me building on the understanding that God is the omnipresent source of all things and could be thought of like an ocean that we are all floating in. Then I heard, "Close but not quite. Rather than think of something dense like an ocean, think of the Source like an energy field that is everything and everywhere." Source, which is more like a cloud than an ocean, then encapsulated bits of itself, like in a balloon or some kind of field. Those distinct pieces within the cloud became us. With the parts of itself that were encapsulated, Source played out a drama that involved us thinking that we were separate from the cloud rather than part of it. In actuality, there is only a thin film between us and the rest of the cloud, and all of us are cloud.

Part of the drama is that we are encouraged to play with different energies, which for the most part are denser than the cloud. One of the rules of the drama is that whatever we think about will be known by Source and sent to us. So if we think about money, we will be sent money. If we think about dogs, we will be sent a dog. Whatever we think about, we will attract like a magnet. Source will send thoughts in a seemingly random way to us, or we can attract the thoughts we want. One way we do that is to emotionally want something. In that case, related thoughts will come. Another way is let our mind go somewhere, and again, related thoughts will follow. We also have the choice to play the game at a higher level by refining and focusing our thoughts and requesting thoughts in a specific area, for example, love or service to nature.

All our thoughts are really the thoughts within the cloud, which is Source. They are not thoughts limited to our encapsulated bubble; thoughts are everywhere. All thoughts are embedded in Source and we are set up as an experiment to see what we will do. We are simply Source experimenting with where we want to take this. So when we talk about Source being non-judgmental, that is the mechanics of it. Everything that we could possibly think of actually comes from Source. We are not coming up with anything new; we are just drawing to us what we want to play with.

When we first start out in the drama, we might be interested in power and sex and the various addictions toward which we all have tendencies. Eventually we get tired of playing with lower-density things because they are inherently not as interesting as higher-density endeavors. We then gravitate toward the higher levels, so rather than having an orgasm physically, our whole body/mind complex experiences ecstasy because we are connected at a higher level to Source. As we focus more on higher-density thoughts, we realize who needs addictions if we can have even more joy without them, so we just do not go there anymore. It is not that one is wrong and one is not, but just that in our own encapsulated piece, we are ready to shift to the higher vibrations.

WE VOLUNTEERED FOR THIS EXISTENCE FROM HIGHER DIMENSIONAL LEVELS

The Healing Light Group, 3-12-16

JOE: We are being called upon to work well beyond just healing the individual that is on the table in front of us and understand that we are working on a planetary and even larger level. At levels beyond what we typically connect into, this work has already been done. This transformation has already occurred at the higher dimensional levels; it just hasn't filtered down yet to the third dimension. It is really a top-down process. Since this has already happened at the higher levels, it is not a question of whether it is going to happen at this level. It is. Our task is just facilitating it in the optimal way. We don't have to think about our work as, "Can we pull this off?" It is already done; we are just facilitating it and bringing it down from the higher levels.

The Healing Light Group, 3-26-16

JOE: This is from a channeled message that said many beings, including probably all of us, volunteered for this existence from higher dimensional levels. We volunteered to incarnate on Earth to help with the almost overwhelming violence, negativity and lack of divine connection here. A reasonable being could have said that we were either foolish or brave to do so because we did not have a guarantee that we could get out again. Just like everybody else who incarnates, we did not carry our memory of prior lifetimes. We do, however, carry some of our prior consciousness at the heart level, so we have an advantage over people who haven't existed at a higher dimension previously.

That being said, we still incarnated with the same human wiring as everybody else, so it's really easy to get caught in lower-level activities and thoughts. This starts with the "Seven Deadly Sins" and extends to numerous other enticements including addictions, worries, anxieties and drives. We had no exemption from the struggles and suffering that afflict every other being on this planet. As a result, a lot of us forgot where we came from, why we came, and what we are doing. Essentially, we got caught in the drama that we came to help fix. If it wasn't for the fact we have so much outside assistance, we would be stuck in the drama just like everybody else. Fortunately, we were not abandoned, and we did not come alone. We might be like paratroopers dropped behind the adversary's lines, but there's an entire support army in back of us. Part of our job is to learn how to let go of the third dimension enticements and impediments so we can model how to transcend this level and create a pathway for others to follow.

AN ENERGY ACTIVATION

Sage, September, 2016

SAGE CONNECTED WITH both Mt. Shasta and an Arcturian craft during this channeling as she and Joe were walking in a field on the way to the Faery Falls near Mt. Shasta.

❖

Part 1 (Mt. Shasta speaks)

MOUNT SHASTA SPEAKING THROUGH SAGE: I live between two worlds. In one I am physical, and in one I am ethereal. You come to me now because you have asked for renewal and to be in touch with higher sources. Look at me, the mountain, as the source that is pointing upward, and know that as high as I go into the universe, you may go and you may connect on hi-dimensional levels with us and with other healing civilizations. They are going to further heal you to make you pure energy. You have a purpose that is not revealed yet. Know that you are unique and carry an energy that allows information to flow to you and through you. It is our gift and the gift from those other civilizations. It will be our greatest pleasure to assist you and for our friends to assist you healing into pure energy. As you flow to us and to them, your vibrations must be much higher. We will work that out; so allow us to do that. We have given all of you as a gift into the world and to those you touch. We are bringing to your world a higher connection and presence of love than you have seen before. You are some of the vehicles that will flow through.

Part 2 (An Arcturian speaks)

SAGE: They are in a craft just above the level that planes would fly because they do not want their presence known today. They are here at this time because there is an energy activation that is going on. They are sending incredible vibrations of love and peace into this mountain and into every tree and person that is here. It is beyond all judgments and will assist our world to remediate what is here today. They are asking that we accept all those who are different from us because we then model that for others. When you stand in the strength of who you are as a true spiritual being accepting love and giving love to all others no matter how different or how many emotions they are showing, you would register in the range of five if your energies could be measured on a Richter scale. The more you do it, the higher your energy vibration will increase. Even if they do not show it, the peace and love that people receive is like a stone that stays with them and builds their spirits beyond their current level. They are giving this to everyone in our group and to everyone who is in a truly spiritual place so that we can walk that journey for them. They will be leaving soon to go to sacred places around the world so this energy and love can spread. They will come back to assist us in bringing in more refined levels of loving and peaceful energy.

JOE: Are they Arcturian?

SAGE: Yes. They are blasting this area now; their energy field is coming through your body into the ground. He says with every conscious step you take, remind yourself that you've been given this gift of loving peaceful energy to share. They are grateful for our assistance in bringing this into our world. They are closing the doors and saying thank you. [Sage chuckled.] They are spinning the ship around in a playful way. He said that is a reminder to always play. They are appreciating and honoring our work. As they are moving away, he is saying that you need to keep clearing your being and working at the highest level you know.

ACCEPT THAT WE ARE WHO WE ARE

The Healing Light Group, 3-8-17

JOHANNA: I think we are all going to realize we are a whole lot more than we knew. We have our brains wrapped around the fact that we are these little people in. The bigger truth is that we are individuals that have been in lifetimes we don't know about. It is time that all of that comes together.

SAGE: I'm picking up that there's fear in some of us about whom we could be, what our ego is going to do with that, and what other people will think of us. We are to remind ourselves that when our ego is saying things like that or like, "now you're really nuts," we are supposed to just let it go and accept that we are who we are. We've all come into this group for a reason.

L.P.: Do you remember saying a few months ago that you felt many of us were on our final lifetime?

JOE: My understanding is that quite possibly everybody in this room started this work eons ago. It was to help with the shift, and this shift is going to occur in our current lifetimes for most of us. I don't know exactly when, but that allows each of us to end our series of incarnations knowing that we finished the task we signed up for. It doesn't mean we can't come back, because there will still be something here after the shift. It is just that for those of us who choose to go on to the next thing, this is an end point. It could well be that many of us will take that opportunity because we're ready for the next thing; it's a choice.

I think most of us came in from sixth density (see the Notes Section), so it is quite a drop down to go to third for all of us. That is part of the reason we struggle and its part of the reason it's so attractive to just go back to where we were.

SAGE: They are telling me for anyone in the group who has any doubts about some of the thing that are being discussed, look at who you were when you entered the group, and look at the changes that you have gone through as a member of the group. That will give you more centeredness on the further evolution of things.

THE OLD NEGATIVE SYSTEM IS CRUMBLING

Sage Part 1, 6-8-17

T*HIS IS THE first of three excerpts prior to a healing session for Joe.*

❖

SAGE: There will be a lot of spiritual energy changes on the Earth. The existing ones will begin to increase in magnitude and new ones will be found. Because of that, some things that seemed impossible are becoming possible. Some of these energies will be cleansing and as they cleanse, they will also create new vibrational frequencies.

Spirit just showed me a dragon flying with someone on its back. They take people with them to show them the truth. He says when you are riding a dragon; you have spiritual sight and see things differently. The dragons create a world that is spiritually strong, and that change will create fear in some people. He says that fear will be rising on the planet in the near future, and when it calms down, the world will go to a deeper level of peace. The dragons are involved in some way.

JOE: I just picked up that terrorist attacks and other negative events are being orchestrated by negatively-oriented fourth-dimensional beings to increase our level of fear. There will be bigger things coming in order to ramp up the fear. What I did not know is that the energies will go to a more solid level of peace once this fear is cleared. Some of these fourth-dimensional beings have been fostering negative activities for thousands of years. That is changing and they won't be allowed to stay here. Some have already left and more will be leaving. They are the top level of control for the entire negative system. When that is dismantled, there will still be much that is negative, but the organizational structure and the black magic component that was holding it together will disappear.

SAGE: I can see that that old negative system was supported at the astral level and it is now crumbling.

JOE: It will become easier for positive energies and beings to influence people at the third-dimensional level going forward. Many people have been duped into supporting that negative agenda. Some of the more negative third-dimensional beings will leave Earth and incarnate elsewhere, and some will think that maybe the new energies offer a better way, and they will shift to a more positive orientation.

SAGE: We need to stand strong and not be in the fear, but be firm in the belief that everything is ok no matter what is going on. Otherwise, we are creating another level of chaos.

JOE: We will all be tested at times and it will be hard to hold a positive understanding. Nevertheless, it will be very important to do so and to hold that positive center like a pillar of light, because many will benefit.

SAGE: We need to remain in that center with no judgement so others will not feel criticized and will be more willing to just stand with us in that light.

A TRANSFORMATIVE COSMIC ENERGY WAVE IS COMING

Sage Part 2, 6-8-17

SAGE: I just saw some beings from The Belt of Orion implanting energy into various places around the world. They said we are safe and there is absolutely no reason for fear during the coming changes. They are saying that we need to help others hold onto that feeling of safety when the time comes. When it does, it will feel like the platform they are standing on is collapsing and that they are falling. There is a bed of white light that goes way down and solemnly flows at the level of the Earth that they will eventually land on. It is amazing how peaceful and calm it feels with no fear anywhere; just total peace.

JOE: Virtually all of our healing group, in particular you, Johanna and I, have been part of an Earth-transforming plan for hundreds of lifetimes. That plan was conceived knowing that a transformative, extremely powerful, cosmic energy wave coming from the center of the galaxy would provide a singular opportunity to affect great positive change.

A group of Lightworkers understood that preparation could maximize the positive impact of the wave and would be critical to affect permanent change. We are already receiving the beginning of that transformational energy and it will get stronger. There might be some very noticeable aspect to it like a flash and things suddenly change, or it might be like heating up a pot of water until you eventually notice it is boiling. I don't know how it will hit, but it will be in a short period of time. By short, it could be five or ten or twenty years; I don't know that part.

That bed of white light you saw earlier is the wave coming in. The role of the Lightworkers is to help humankind be ready. This involves the releasing of negative energies and helping people become more selfless. There have been great teachers over the millennium to help with this and a lot of those teachers were Lightworkers in that group. There has also been the removal of some pretty negative beings by fifth and sixth densities Lightworkers as part of the plan.

SAGE: Those Lightworkers who have prepared will be used, even if that preparation was in a prior lifetime. They know they must be pure light. If they are hooking into the fear aspect of things, then they are hooking into partial darkness. Even though there may be much in turmoil or much that is negative, they must stay strong and be the light for others.

JOE: We talked earlier about the group members being pillars of light in the chaos, and that is the same as what you are saying. You cannot be a pillar of light if you get hooked by the negative or the fear.

JOE: There is a piece that I think is true regarding the cosmic wave. The shift that's occurring has been called by others, "the shift of the ages." It happens every once in a while and is a wave of energy from the great Central Sun in the center of the galaxy. Everything it reaches gets upgraded to the next higher density. We will be upgrading on Earth from the third to the fifth density because we were not ready for the last shift of the ages and we have the opportunity to catch up to where we could have been.

WE ARE ALL ONE BEING

Sage Part 3, 6-8-17

JOE: When a channeled message comes through, the sender uses the framework of the person receiving, so a fundamentalist Christian might hear a message regarding devils and angels, while we might hear the same message in terms of higher and lower vibrational energies. It is just different terminology. Separate from that, there is a piece of great significance that not one of us in the group has truly absorbed, which is that we are all one being. Once that knowledge becomes an operating principal and we just know it, everything changes. Until that point, we have the enemy within, and the enemy within is keeping us from understanding that. It is the part of us that thinks we are just an individual. At different times, we have each gotten past that and we all know that we are beings of light, but it is not our everyday conscious operational awareness.

SAGE: Not unless I am around people like you and Johanna where that connection is present.

JOE: Even then, I do not reach the level where I understand we are one being.

SAGE: I can get there once in a while.

JOE: We have all touched it enough to know it is true, so I have an intellectual understanding from memory, but it is not what I see when I open my eyes.

SAGE: They told me I need to tell you about an experience I had and to make it available to others. It began when I went to see a sleep specialist and she wanted to know my entire background. I told her my story, which was very traumatic in many respects, and she asked if it left me anxious or depressed. I told her no and she was shaking her head, and then asked me about how my family members died. I told her two died in separate fires, and she said, "Oh my God, are you ok?" I said yes and she asked me more questions about my family and she's just looked at me with concern and said, "Who supports you?" I said I support myself, and she said, "What about religion?" I said I am a very spiritual individual, but I don't do religion.

I told her that she needed to understand that I like myself and am ok with myself. Those difficult experiences affected many aspects of my life and helped me to create a lot of very good things, but that is not who I am. She said, "I don't understand." I told her I went through that life, I like who I am, I even love myself, I like where I live, I like what I do, I have friends, I can be alone or I can be with whoever I want. I don't have to be around other people and I don't need to cling to people. She said, "I don't know what to say. You are unique, I guess."

I went out for a walk that night and J.M. from our group happened to call. Spirit said to stop, stand on the grass and explain to J.M. what happened with the sleep specialist. I did, and as soon as I finished, a huge wave of energy came through me into the earth and then came back up and went out. When it went out, it was like, oh my God, I am one with the trees. I can feel this unity going on and on and I am it. I am one with everything.

Spirit said that is where people need to get to, the place where they are totally okay with themselves. Then they can experience not only oneness, but also much more joy. They said that was an example of where people need to be.

A HEART CONNECTION TO THE SOURCE

The Healing Light Group, 10-28-17

SAGE HAD JUST *connected with high-dimensional beings from a pink nebula in space.*

❖

SAGE: They said to take our energy and touch into that nebula because there are beings there who are asking to work with us. They have not touched with us before, but they said due to the chaos in our world, they were asking permission to come now.

A BEING FROM THE NEBULA SPEAKING THROUGH SAGE: We are what you would call very high beings. We are here to enlarge your hearts, to enlarge your auric fields, and to assist you through every moment of the day to hold the space that your world needs now. You work hard at it, and with your permission, we are going to help you do that in a way that it is no longer work for you. We will assist you to be in alignment with the One, and that will then be who you are. We are grateful to be able to be of assistance to help you and allow you to get to that space. We tell you there is no doubt that you can all do this.

We have great, great gratitude for allowing us to enter within your space and allowing us to assist and guide you to be totally in alignment with the One, and to assist with the next phase of your Earth journey. We know the sacred people that you are, and we honor that. We honor that in your physical form and we honor that in your spiritual form. Know that when and if you choose to do this, and we hope you all do, that you will be changed and others will sense that there is something in you that will feel good. But if a person is out of alignment with their true self and in a very negative space, they will be uncomfortable. You will carry an energy connection to the One and to the Source, and you will carry incredible love for all things that will be felt by others in your vibrational field, even though they do not know what it is. You have agreed to do this across many lifetimes. I need to tell you now that this is a very powerful and sacred alignment. And again, I tell you that it is your choice.

MULTIPLE GROUP MEMBERS: I choose to do this.

DAN: I took my dog for a walk today and it was just so amazing. So many people were stopping and talking and I'm thinking everyone is so friendly. People were coming off their porch to talk. I just got a message that's all it is; that all you need to do is just be nice to people. That is all that is required.

H.M.: If you can still communicate with them, can you ask them if the next phase they refer to is related to planetary alignments?

THE BEING SPEAKING THROUGH SAGE: It is more than the next phase of your human world. This alignment will never go away, but you will receive others on top of it.

SAGE: He is showing me there is where we were, and here we become aligned. It's incredible love and there's this powerful energy that comes down that is connecting into the Source. He says that depending on what occurs upon your earth and how integral you choose to be, that will identify when the next alignment will come in. He says it's like having this being come, and then that being will come, and then this other being will come, and then another being will come. They will always be changing the vibration of you for the better.

THE BEING SPEAKING THROUGH SAGE: I need to tell you that

it is critically important that you understand that to do this, to come into alignment, you do nothing. You do not need to struggle or fix; you do nothing but allow us to work through whatever your resistance is and bring you into alignment with the Source, with the One. It is important that you have total trust and allow us to be with you and allow us to work through you and assist you to release, to let go, and to do whatever is necessary for you to be in this alignment. So know that is what you need to be and that is where you need to be. I say again, do nothing. It is not your job. Accept the grace and accept the alignment and then walk forward knowing you are one with love. We would never hurt you.

The group was talking for approximately 10 minutes about what just occurred when Sage interrupted.

SAGE: He just said stop.

THE BEING SPEAKING THROUGH SAGE: What did we tell you? Looking for explanations takes you out of love and puts you in the brain, which is useless for the work. Open yourselves now and allow us to energetically connect with your heart, and allow us to be with you. Shut off your brain and ego, which has doubt. Just be! We ask you, as we fill you with this alignment to the Source and One, to take your hands and face them into the room allowing our energy to fill the room. As we leave, we tell you we have created an alignment in you, and we have created sacred space in you. We bypassed your brain and your ego to do this. We, through you, created incredible sacred space of light and love within this room. Thank you.

SAGE: He said as he was leaving that you can never destroy the sacred space that was created in you and the sacred space that was created in this room. That will always stay; some of it will dissipate, but a portion of it will always stay. Sacred space cannot be destroyed; it can be added to.

JOE: I know when he told me to get out of my mind; I thought, how? Then I remembered a very simple mantra I used sometimes. It is saying "light" with the in breath and "love" with the out breath. It just repeats: light, love, light, love, as long as desired. I was able to do that, and that took me back to the heart.

DAN: There is a great saint in India, Nisargadatta Maharaj, who is noted to be one of the beings who went the whole distance. He was asked, what was your path that brought you to this? He said that his Guru simply told him to concentrate on his own beingness, so that is what he did. That is all he said. So when they are saying just concentrate on being, there is almost like a vibration that you feel, like your life force or something. He says just rest in that; don't do anything else and everything will just take care of itself from that space.

SAGE: Somebody new is talking to me and is saying, "You are the light of the world, as all could be. Not all chose to be the light of the world. To be the light of the world, you have had to change. Not everyone chooses change now, but they will. So those you are in angst with, just voice change, because that is what you send. We see with eyes that you don't know, and we flow into spaces where you don't go. We leave behind seeds that any can touch. It is always their choice."

THREE DRAGONS

Johanna, 1-22-18

T̲ʜɪs ᴛᴏᴏᴋ ᴘʟᴀᴄᴇ *during a healing session for Joe.*

❖

JOE: You said I had three dragons come in.

JOHANNA: Three dragons came in pretty quickly to take us for a journey. At some point, we were transferred from dragon to meteors because we went beyond where the dragons could go. It seems like your energy just needed to flow. You were taking off very quickly and it was a nice ride, like we were just cruising through the universe. It felt to me like you were directing the path somewhat with your mind, but it didn't really feel like you had a destination. It seemed like a curious journey of fact-finding. You were just checking out space, outer space.

When I was back here with you on the table, it felt like they were clearing a lot of old patterns and energy. There were very thick tree-like roots coming from your feet, like old roots that needed some clearing, so they did some polishing and stuff. There is better transmission between your feet and the soil, so you might find yourself being able to ground more easily. The throat charka also needed extra clearing.

JOE: It seems like there's no end to clearing.

JOHANNA: Right. Well, we have cleared many timelines, whether it is lifetimes or years, but we've got thousands of lifetimes.

JOE: And they all have to be cleared?

JOHANNA: They all have to be cleared, so it's a process. It feels like the more we pull out, the more energy we have to work on the other stuff ourselves.

JOE: Well, that is terrific. Thank you. I have been kind of the sluggish lately.

JOHANNA: That is what it felt like.

JOE: That has been going on for a few years, but more so lately. Part of it is no doubt age, but part of it is that I feel worn out.

JOHANNA: I think a lot has to do with the energy that is changing so rapidly within us and around us. We just need to pay attention to it and give it what it needs. I think if we polled the members of the healing group, we would probably have at least 95% of them saying they just can't do it the way they used to. I've been tapping into the fifth dimension and just asking for assistance. I feel like we're about 20% third dimension and 80% fifth dimension, and we need to start making the cognitive change to be there as well.

JOE: When my eyes are closed, I'm not third dimension. I'm also much less interested in third-dimensional stuff. I follow politics because it is like a movie to me, but I'm not attached to the outcome.

JOHANNA: That's a big step because the more we get attached to the outcomes, the more we stay in third dimension. I'm finding it easier to be in a space of love and joy and contentment with being third dimension when you know you're fifth dimension, if that makes sense. I just find it nice to take a dip into the fifth dimension energy.

STEP UP FROM THE WORDS OF LOVING ALL TO BEING THE LOVE OF ALL

Sage, 1-25-18

T*HIS CHANNELING OCCURRED when Sage was helping Joe arrange the crystals in his study. Johanna came over a little later.*

❖

SAGE: Spirit wants you to pull one of these cards. They said it will add to your understanding.

JOE: The card I pulled was Mary Magdalene. It says, "The teacher awakens."

SAGE: I'm going to call forth Mary Magdalene. That is interesting; she says this needs to be recorded.

MARY MAGDALENE THROUGH SAGE: "I come forth asking you to be aware of balance in every aspect of your life. Know that the work you have done has created good and will continue beyond you. Awaken yourself as a teacher who is wise in the silence and able to speak truth when that is needed. Know that all are not ready for our messages. You go beyond self as you accept and acknowledge the oneness of self with me and with others who have walked where you all walk. Feel that you are not separate and know when you create from your inner being, you draw from the wellspring of all life.

I bring many blessings to those who approach me. Those who

come to me are ready to step up their life's journey to acknowledge on a different level who they are and what love actually is in this world. I send from my heart to your heart and into the heart of all beings: human, animals, and your planet. My love is not restricted and is open and flowing in massive amounts. I ask you to step up from the words of loving all to being the love of all things. I energize that level within you and you can transfer this energy out. I am the light as you are the light; I am love as you are love, and I am one with spirit as you are one with the spiritual aspects of you and me. Do not see separation because we are one. It's only when you see me as not you that you stay in the third dimensional aspects of life. I energize and I give you the vibrations of love and being one with me and being one with and for the world."

SAGE: It is our physical thinking that restricts us. I am getting the message that you are to be aware when Mary Magdalene is with you and you are to allow her to be you. Also, obstacles are being removed.

JOE: There is an image that may be helpful for understanding this. For our incarnations in this dimension, which are innumerable, there has always been a wall of separation between us and others. We have lived so many lifetimes that we think that's normal. It's a wall, although sometimes people think of it as a mist or veil, but it's a barrier for most. That barrier is what Mary Magdalene is telling us to cross, to diminish, to forget. There is something that can help us with that. The dragon is here and offering to just burn the wall down, just burn it. The only thing we have to do is say yes, go for it, burn that wall down. They will help us, that is, all three of us. That is why Tucker growled at the black origami dragon earlier tonight. The dragon had been energized by our earlier work in a way that Tucker noticed when he came into the room, and he was a little worried about that dragon energy.

JOE: Light, Lighter and Lightest are chuckling at us because they know we think we are doing this for the first time, and we think it is some big thing that we are doing here. But we have been well beyond this point. There was a reason why we came to this planet and the third dimension, and we're close to fulfilling that reason.

THE LIGHT IS THE SAME IN ALL OF US

The Healing Light Group, 3-10-18

JOHANNA: WHEN we use language to talk about what we're doing, we need to be careful of the words we use. When you say that we're sending energy, it is more accurate to say that we are sending our intention, and the energy follows the intention. Even when I am physically standing next to a client, I am again sending my intention and focusing on my intention. The energy does what it needs to do. They have been telling us for a long time to get out of the way and let them do the work. I always send my intention to do whatever is in the client's highest and best. It's a big difference, but it's really just reframing.

SAGE: Energy follows intention.

L.P.: I have always felt that.

JOHANNA: When I'm working with somebody, I definitely feel the energy coming through me, but I don't feel like it's my energy. I don't want to give away my energy. It is the universal energy that really does the work. We don't know what is the highest and best for the client. If it is time for them to go, then let them go, even if it may not be what we personally want.

JOE: Maybe I should say something. It started with a clear message from Spirit that came in several weeks ago when Sage came to my house to help arrange the crystals in my study. We were talking about sending energy, and the message came, "Don't send, just be." Be the love, be the light. During the channeling, Sage went somewhere very deep and was groggy afterward for a long period. I called Johanna to come over and help Sage come back, and then Johanna went deep into some sort of trance state and also was groggy afterwards. It was all revolving around the basic idea of "Don't do. Be." "You are the message." We all looked at one another asking what to do with this guidance, because it takes things to a level we were not prepared for and don't really know how to implement.

Then another related piece came in two days ago. I was meditating in the morning and trying to work with Mary Magdalene and Jesus to send healing energy. Usually when I did this, I would go up through the chakras in my body to the crown chakra or the third eye and try to connect with them. That method had worked well for me frequently. The idea in my mind is that I am trying to get clear enough or high enough that I can reach them. This of course implies that they are out there and I am in here, and it also means I completely ignored the message described above.

This morning, however, my usual meditation technique resulted in the metaphysical equivalent of a slap across the face along with the message, "Don't do that." Instead, go inside into your heart and connect with them from the inside. Go inside and get to the point where there is no distinction between you and them; where you are Mary Magdalene, you are the love, you are Jesus. Go inward and connect that way. I did as spirit suggested and there was a tremendous feeling of love and light.

Throughout all of this, the understanding was that the information I am receiving is also for our group. I believe that to the extent that we can do it, this is now the preferred method to connect with higher vibrational beings. They also said it's going to meet with resistance, so do what you can.

Remember a couple years ago when we were given the concept of one-touch-healing and it was a leap from what we used to do? This is another leap. So the message is, "Be the light; be the love."

To rephrase it, "I am the light; I am love." From there, things happen; we don't to even need to have intention. What needs to happen just happens.

JOHANNA: I was chuckling when you said "Just be" because of what happened when I was at the hospital and we were using the letter board to communicate with Dan. It was a struggle for him to use the board and on two different occasions he simply spelled out the word "Be." T.P. got the impression that part of the reason for Dan's coma was to get messages from the other side for all of us.

JOE: So he is ahead of us. Maybe he's the one pulling us all forward.

JOHANNA: I think Joe is right about what we are supposed to be doing. This is just the tip of the iceberg of what we are going to be asked to do this year. 2018 is going to be a year that explodes with the shifting of energies in the universe. I think we are all being challenged to really step into a new space, and everyone from the Healing Light Group is meant to be in it. I feel like it's going to be a whole new way of operating, but it may not be for everybody

SAGE: The message that came to me for 2018 is, "Don't resist."

JOE: There is one more part of the message which, at its core, is that we are one with Jesus and Mary Magdalene, and of course that means everyone. It is not that we are special; it is just the nature of things. We are one; we're not different. That is the message they are trying to help us understand and imbibe. We are one.

JOHANNA: We all have the light, everybody has light. If we go in to find that light, the light is the same in all of us, and that is where we can all be one.

SAGE: When I went over to Joe's that night, I had an experience I have never had. When I walked into the study to help arrange his crystals, I was immediately one with them. I didn't even hear them talking to me like I usually do. It's just that I was them and they were me, and I knew where everything needed to go. I didn't do anything; when I pick up a crystal, my hand just knew where to put it for the maximum synergy among the crystals.

EXPANDING TO THE SIZE OF THE SUN

Johanna, 6-27-18

THIS TOOK PLACE *during a healing session for Joe.*

❖

JOHANNA: So when I came to the top of your head, it had already started dissolving and mingling and then it suddenly went expansive. I got pushed up against the wall and it just took me somewhere. At one point it was like I was the sun or the moon, and I floated back and forth between the two. That's the energy we carry now and that we need to see ourselves as. It is very obvious that we have been seeing ourselves as very minute when we need to see ourselves as these big universal beings.

JOE: Okay.

JOHANNA: One time while I was more sun energy, I was in the room and your energy was on top of mine and just drawing that sun energy into your energy. Then your energy filled the room, then it filled the building, then it filled the city and then it filled the planet. Both of our energies just kept expanding up to that point. It is like the old way of doing things is useless.

JOE: So we need to think on a whole different scale.

JOHANNA: So when they say, get out of the way, they mean it. We really need to start thinking of our bodies as just barriers.

JOE: Okay.

JOHANNA: It feels like we are going to be shedding that restriction and be able to move beyond our bodies. I could feel energy coming from my chest, not from just the heart chakra. It is like all of the chakras were coming together and then coming out through the heart chakra. At that point I heard it was all love and love is what we exchange. But the biggest thing was just how expansive we can be without losing ourselves.

JOE: I felt more peaceful than ever at the deepest possible level.

JOHANNA: I am not quite sure where we were, but we were connected wherever we were.

WORKING TOGETHER

The Healing Light Group Part 1, 6-30-18

THIS TOOK PLACE at an outdoor social gathering of the Healing Light Group.

❖

JOE: So those clouds are angels.

SAGE: You can see their bodies between those branches and their wings are up there. (Sage is now pointing at a different part of the sky.) Those energies over there are dragon and ET energies and they are getting closer to Earth and closer together. They are communicating with one another. Notice the dragon taking shape in that cloud.

JOE: Yes, it is a dragon.

SAGE: Do you see it, Mark?

MARK: Oh yes. I also see another dragon over there.

SAGE: The dragon is talking about fire. Mark, are you picking up on anything?

MARK: I see something growing out of the ashes. It is part of the cycle. When you burn down something, like a forest, new growth comes in.

SAGE: I sense the energy of a burning fire; I think that is what they are energetically doing right now.

MARK: They are breaking down old energies for new ones to come in.

SAGE: That is one of the reasons why it is important that people pay attention to where they are energetically, because if they remain in negativity too long, the burning and breaking down of old energies will not occur.

SAGE: This is interesting; the others are kind of protecting the dragon energies.

JOE: You are saying the ETs and the angels are protecting the dragon energies.

SAGE: Yes.

JOE: So the angels, the ETs and the dragons are all working together.

SAGE: Yes. They are saying it is a critical time and we need to work together. They are modeling what we need to do here. All of those groups are also releasing energy to us.

JOE: So they are modeling working together, which is what we need to be doing with other groups here?

SAGE: They are telling me it is like misfiring brain synapses. Other groups are doing the same thing we are doing, but we are cross-firing right now. We need to set our intent that we are in coordination with them and that we are all working together. That way, the synapses will all firing in sync. If we keep that as our intention, we will be better able to connect with the energies of the other groups.

WE CANNOT MINIMIZE WHO WE ARE

The Healing Light Group Part 2, 6-30-18

SAGE: WHAT he just said to me is there is dragon energy, ET energy and angelic energy. It is like there are levels and when we are ready, the energy levels and beings will appear. He says there is space between each world that is very high energy for creating only the good. They're asking us to acknowledge the gift and the power of that energy each time we encounter it. As we do that and are willing to be of service to it, then more will come forward, but not until they feel that we are energetically and consciously ready.

JOE: There is a piece about being ready that ties in with this. I had a treatment with Johanna a few days ago. One of the things that happened to both of us was our bodies expanded first to the size of the room, then the building, then the city. We each expanded in size until we were the size of the planet or the size of the sun. We need to have a new understanding. We are not small and cannot work with these new energies until we acknowledge that about ourselves. So think about the being the size of the planet or the sun with the energy to affect everything in the system, as opposed to being where we have been. We cannot work with those higher energies unless we change our mindset.

SAGE: He says it is not always about us using the energy; it is also about us connecting and being with the energy. As you said, we have to have a different level of awareness and understanding and we cannot minimize who we are. That is one of the reasons they told me when I am seeing Jesus, or Mary Magdalene or Mother Mary, that I have to say it aloud because we have to be integral with whatever we are knowing, doing or being. That tells them we acknowledge that we are working at a different level. When we acknowledge that or we get into the space where we can be in tune, they get very happy. Similarly, their letting us sense their energies is their way of acknowledging us.

Joe: What I am getting is that we are part of a multidimensional team, and that we have a role that is just as important as that of any other team member. The fact that we happen to be foot soldiers in the third dimension doesn't lessen our value nor does it preclude our larger self also playing an important role.

Sage: The fact that you talk to dragons and I talk to other beings or the fact that you and Johanna receive spiritual information doesn't make us different from others. It is just that we have allowed ourselves to be honest and integral with whom we are. They are saying that is what every one of us has to do.

Joe: Thank you.

Sage: They said you are welcome. They are saying that diminishing yourself does not help.

Joe: It is not just diminishing ourselves that we need think about. It also means realizing that we are larger and more powerful than we previously thought by an enormous amount. I do not have a good idea what a soul is, but I did not think of my soul as the size of the sun, so I need to change my thinking.

BECOME ONE WITH THE EARTH

Sage and Johanna Part 1, 7-13-18

THIS TOOK PLACE *following a healing session for Joe.*

❖

JOHANNA: I heard that we really need to focus on appreciation as well as gratitude, and that there is a difference. It is expressing appreciation for the people we work with, the guides we work with, the energies we work with, as well as the gratitude for being able to receive.

SAGE: What I am getting is that we need to appreciate the fact that we are able to do this work. Just honoring and appreciating everything they do for us and the gifts they give us that helps us open up.

JOE: I should probably tell you what just happened to me. I opened myself up as much as I possibly could and in came Mary Magdalene, Mother Mary and Jesus. They said we are all one inside you now. We are just one inside now.

JOHANNA: I felt this huge teepee of energy. I call it a teepee because it is like an upside down funnel of energy over you that just came down like a whoosh.

JOE: Years ago, the energies of Archangel Michael came in that way. So it is not the first time this has happened, but it seems like a higher level than I am used to. I think the trick is to understand that inside you, it is all there.

JOHANNA: We just need to allow it. Being that expansive open self that we talked about last time allows us to tap into that and recognize that it is there. When I have been doing massages lately, I have been going into an almost trancelike state, and there are times my hands will disappear and I can't move. It feels like my hands are going into different dimensions. It comes back to normal after a while, but it seems like there is something going on deeper than just tissue release.

JOE: I was just told why grounding is so important. Do you remember the vortex in Lake Placid that suddenly just shot out of the floor when we held the Healing Light Group meeting there? Then later, we connected to some energy at the base of Whiteface Mountain that stayed with us for about a mile as we walked back before returning into the ground.

JOHANNA: Yes.

JOE: It's us. That energy was us. We are the vortex energies.

JOHANNA: Cool.

SAGE: That is why they always appear.

JOE: That is why we have to ground, because we are deeply connected with the Earth energies. We have to become one with the Earth itself.

JOHANNA: It feels like just sinking roots into the ground is old school.

JOE: Right. This needs to be like merging with the planet Earth.

JOHANNA: I am being told that there are many ways to do this. You can see and feel yourself wrapped up in grass, sinking into the earth, on a beach, on a mountain or whatever it is you connect with. It is about being one with or immersed in the Earth, not just being connected by little tentacles.

JOE: We are only beginning to glimpse who we are and what our role in this whole transition is. It changed everything I previously thought when: 1) we expanded to the size of the sun, 2) I realized that the powerful vortex of energy in Lake Placid was us, and 3) the Mother Mary, Mary Magdalene and Jesus energies came in. We are also connected to the Christ energies to the extent we can work with them in this dimension and are fully connected with them in our larger selves.

JOHANNA: That golden teepee doesn't leave me. I don't really even need to ask. It is just when I start working, it is there.

JOE: The deal is that although we are relatively unique in terms of humans right now, we are not unique in the slightest in terms of human potential. We are simply models for others and assisting with the movement of others. There are plenty of others who do this as well.

JOHANNA: I think rather than being in awe at everything that happens, we need to expect that amazing new things are going to, and that it is just normal stuff now.

JOE: It is just normal. As we awaken to the higher levels, we need to understand that is what the higher levels are. It is nothing special. It is just that most people in this dimension, including us, are not aware of those levels.

JOHANNA: It is like power windows in your car. It is normal now, but we all played with the button when we first got them. Were you recording this?

JOE: About the power windows? It will be part of this forever and ever. (All laughing)

JOE: Speaking of cars, I realized driving over here something about how the pace of the transition seems interminable to me. My guide said for everybody else, it is going at breakneck speed, and they can just barely stand it. So it is just a different perspective.

OUR SOUL IS OUR GUIDE

Sage and Johanna Part 2, 7-13-18

JOHANNA: When I go back to Light, Lighter, and Lightest and how you (Joe) identified them as our respective souls. I see them as working in different dimensions. I can see Sage being Light because she's reaching down and pulling people in because people understand how she works with the other energies. I'm in the middle taking people from her and sending them to you. You're in the highest dimension because you're the way-shower. You are the one connecting and moving up and we're climbing up the ladder with you.

JOE: What are souls then?

JOHANNA: I see souls as the energetic part of us and the part that can expand to be as large as the sun. I think of my soul as my energetic connection to the universe.

SAGE: It is the part of us that started at creation.

JOHANNA: What is the purpose of the soul?

SAGE: I just heard for us to learn to be all that we can be. It helps push us to experience different things.

JOHANNA: I just heard the word "leader."

JOE: So the soul is a leader.

JOHANNA: It manages our movements, not physical movements, but our movement through life. It helps us to see what we need to see. I think intuition is connected to the soul and that it guides us to fulfil our purpose and remain connected with God.

SAGE: I just heard that our soul is the guide that arranges for us to meet whom we need to meet, be where we need to be, do this, and do that, because those are the experiences that are completing our purpose. Our soul is helping guide us through all of those experiences.

JOE: So the soul manages all the incarnations?

JOHANNA: I would think so.

DRAGONS ARE THE SERAPHIM

Johanna, 12-4-18

This took place *following a healing session for Joe during which he drew the Alpha Dragon card from a deck of spiritual message cards. It said the Alpha Dragon harnesses the Divine masculine power of creation and carries Archangel Metatron's highest light.*

❖

JOHANNA: When we were down in Lemuria, I saw a lot of chains and shackles and it went back lifetime after lifetime after lifetime. Spirit was clearing stuff from each lifetime and the chains were falling off. Then there was a little space on your back that opened up and this grief and sadness came pouring out like Niagara Falls. As we worked through the lifetimes, that kept getting smaller to the point where it closed up. There was no darkness except for the color of the chains and shackles, and they were dark black. Everything else seemed to be lighter blue. That part was holding you in a good space, and was removing the old belief systems and patterns from many lifetimes. Once it got finished with that, everything just went bright white, like fresh snow sparkling on a pristine field. It was a healing of your past, present and future. It was like a rototiller going through your energy fields just bringing stuff up so it could be healed.

JOE: Thank you. So I drew the Alpha Dragon card.

JOHANNA: Yes. I drew it a few weeks ago.

JOE: I learned something about dragons just last night. The dragons are the seraphim. William Henry was speaking about it on the Gaia TV channel. He is an art historian that looks at old artifacts, paintings and antiquities of different kinds and talks about what they mean.

JOHANNA: I had heard that about the dragons.

JOE: It is interesting to me that somebody in the Catholic Church knew about this stuff because the seraphim are mentioned at every mass as a category of angel.

JOHANNA: Of course they knew.

WE ARE A PLATOON OF LIGHTWORKERS

The Healing Light Group, 12-8-2018

M<small>EMBERS OF THE</small> *group had reported feeling the presence of ethereal beings in the room and were speculating on what was happening.*

❖

JOE: I know a piece about what's happening. We are being presented like a platoon at a reviewing stand. We are a platoon of Lightworkers and we're being honored with this review and at the same time, receiving blessings that upgrade us. It is a very high-level recognition of the group and what we do. Part of this is for us to acknowledge just who we are and that we don't play an ordinary role. We are an assembled team and individually have all brought much to the table. Collectively, we are more than that.

JOHANNA: Will we get special rings that light? I want to be Green Lantern [laughter from everyone].

JOHANNA: It felt like they were creating an additional bond between us, and that our connection to one another was being energized and activated. It felt like we were one being when we were told to stand next to each other earlier, and that energy went to the entire group even if they were not physically present. Even though I was standing just inches from the people on my sides and in back of me, I could feel other beings between us. For a moment while we standing there, that is all there was of the universe.

JOE: The message I am getting is that we function as a group. The individual is becoming less and less important no matter what particular skills or connections they have. It is the group function that is paramount.

JOHANNA: It doesn't matter if somebody is physically present or not; they are here.

JOE: I think Judy and Dan (the two group members that died) are equally here.

JOHANNA: Absolutely. They are probably leading the parade.

N.M.: As Laura would say, "They don't have to be present to win" [laughter from everyone].

N.M.: It felt like we were a flock flying in a chevron formation in murmuration with H.L. in the lead.

SAGE: When flocks fly and the one in front goes to the back, another one always steps up and they never lose their formation or direction. It says to me, like in a flock, everybody is as important as everybody else.

JOE: It says to me, you can't even get out of this group by dying [laughter from everyone].

THE POWER OF THE HEART CONSCIOUSNESS IS IMMENSE

The Healing Light Group, 1-26-19

H.M.: ANGELS, spirits, guides, masters, loved ones, constellation friends, dragon friends: we welcome you and all other beings in the universe who feel called to come and join us. We welcome you all.

L.P.: Do you feel like somebody is right here (pointing to an empty space next to her)? I had to move over (laughter by many).

JOE: Ok, now I feel some kind of energetic presence.

JOHANNA: Yes, there is something unusual here.

L.P.: I don't know if I should sit down [more laughter].

JOE: The same with me. It feels like I would be sitting on somebody if I did.

Joe passes around a meteorite.

JOE: I am being told to go ahead with my thought, which has to do with this meteorite. This was in my basement because Sage told me the energy was too dark to keep in my office. Spirit said to bring it here today. I asked why and received this question in response. "Where do you think it came from?" I answered the asteroid belt probably and heard, "What do you think that was?" I said a planet, and the next question was, "What do you think is left energetically after a planet blows up?" I said a big mess, and they said, "Yes." I thought if the group chooses to, we could work with that energy.

L.P.: That stone is pulsing.

Joe: Just to make this story a little bit more negative. The planet may have blown up because of a war and not just some accidental thing. There may have been some pretty nasty beings on that planet, and they well may be here at this point. I think some of the real negative forces on our planet are related to that planet blowing up. I don't think the survivors necessarily said we better change our ways because we blew up our planet. I think they just looked for another planet to dominate.

H.M.: It feels like a percolating energy in the stone, like a volcano about to erupt.

T.P.: I felt a buzzing.

L.P.: I felt cold, dark outer space.

The group decides to work with this energy and sets up a multi-layer crystal grid to assist.

Joe: I think we need to call in assistance.

L.P.: There is a dragon coming in, hovering.

Johanna: There is more than one dragon here.

L.P.: The black dragon knows the story.

Johanna: He is taking us back to the beginning of time.

Joe: We are being asked to hold the energy of peace in our hearts and to connect to one another and to all the beings assisting so we create one large heart consciousness.

L.P.: This stone is symbolic of darkness within each of us. We are being asked to choose either to stay aligned with that darkness or to consciously break free using the collective heart consciousness to assist us when we are drawn to low vibrational energy, darkness, despair, bad habits or old habits. At those times, we can choose to either align with that low vibrational energy or connect with the heart consciousness.

JOHANNA: The conscious heart energy is shifting the heaviness and dark energy within this stone in order to show us how we can elevate our own lower energies.

L.P.: The power of the heart consciousness is immense, much greater than any darkness. The more beings that are joined to it, the more power it has, and the more who are awakened, the more power it has. I just keep hearing that we always have a choice.

Approximately 10 minutes of quiet group energy work

UNIDENTIFIED VOICES: That was amazing [with murmurs of agreement].

JOE: I saw the heart consciousness like a sun almost, and it was truly amazing. The meteorite was inside of it representing the whole planet that was destroyed. Basically, the souls of the beings on that planet are going to be exposed to that heart energy, which has very strong feelings of peace. It is giving the souls the experience of peace as an alternative path for them to take instead of the warring path they had been on forever. So this was an exposure to an alternative. They still have choice, but at least now it is a bit more of an informed choice. They can feel what peace would be like.

JOHANNA: What I saw when the dragon took us back to the beginning of time was this book that felt holy, like a sacred document. They were flipping through the pages going backwards to a period of time we can't even conceptualize. It felt like it was before creation and there was a negative, dark heavy kind of energy that started everything. I think we just provided knowledge of the alternative energy of peace. It is making a new start possible with the knowledge there is a choice that can be made.

L.P.: The meteorite is not pulsing anymore.

T.P.: It feels calmer.

L.P.: It feels like just a rock now.

JOHANNA: It feels like it has the energy of creation now and there is more of a positive spin to it.

JOE: I am getting that there is a spirit connected to the stone, almost like a black knight in armor. It was focused on power and negative energy since its beginning. Now it is saying that it sees this other option and will consider it. He wasn't making any promises, but he did say he would help with the creative pieces.

JOHANNA: The stone still has some Darth Vader energy, but it doesn't seem quite as aggressive or threatening now. It is not quite playful, but like it is at least considering it.

THE NATURE OF THE SOUL

Johanna, 1-29-19

THIS TOOK PLACE *during a healing session for Joe.*

❖

JOHANNA: I am feeling something shifting within your chest right now.

JOE: Yes.

JOHANNA: It feels like heart consciousness. It feels like they (spiritual beings) are planting a garden and there are very specific rows with threads or something being laid in the rows and then covered up. Now they're doing rows that are perpendicular and a little deeper. The threads are different colors with hues that are very brilliant. Now they are going back to the original direction, only off to the side a little bit. They may be making something like a three dimensional Metatron's cube (see the Notes Section). Does that resonate with you at all?

JOE: Something is happening. My physical heart is connecting to the higher heart. It is the same heart consciousness that we were in the other day at the Healing Light Group meeting.

JOHANNA: Right. It feels like the crystalline body (see the Notes Section) is needed to bridge the gap between the two hearts.

JOE: Okay, that makes perfect sense, and I certainly welcome that.

JOHANNA: Seeing Metatron's cube shows me that the crystalline body is taking form. It is about two feet off your chest now and is radiating from the center of your chest in all directions. I feel your physical body dissolving. It's just expanding and kind of disappearing. The particles that I can still see look like silver glitter just floating through the air.

JOE (NOW IN A PARTIAL VISION STATE): That is the soul.

JOHANNA: Yes. I see it scrolling through your lifetimes like microfilm, and it is erasing all of the karmic debt and the entire struggle. It is elevating you to a place of peace, grace, love, and enlightenment and is fine-tuning your ability to perceive and understand the true meaning behind the words and behind language. It is like you are cutting through the language and getting right to the pure essence, the holy meanings.

JOE: Those lifetimes are just thoughts, explorations.

JOHANNA: I just heard truths.

JOE: From the soul level, creation is this beautiful space to explore, and the incarnations are just thoughts of explorations. They have no weight to them.

JOHANNA: Right. This is where the duality falls off. There is no good or bad. There is no right or wrong. It is just experiences. It is just there.

JOE: Exactly.

JOHANNA: Now I heard fullness.

JOE: The soul knows it is part of the divine creation. It is just right there seeing it, exploring.

JOHANNA: I feel like there is only one true soul, and we all are that soul. It is like we are a piece of God, but God is soul. We all have our own little understanding of or connection to our soul; we are not separate. When you get to you where you are right now being so dispersed and just having your little glitter floating around, that is all within the larger space called soul. So we are all intermingling pieces in the soul. Like glitter madness [laughter].

At this point, there were ten minutes of quiet energy work during which Joe had a vision in which he merged with his soul. He tells Johanna about it.

JOE: Thank you. After you were quiet, a bright light like a sun, but not as solid as the sun, became visible on most of the screen in my mind. That was God who is simultaneously all that is and the Creator of all that is. Before that, there was a scene of space filled with souls. The understanding came as I was there in my soul that I have had all these explorations, some of which manifested as incarnations. They were just explorations. You learn or experience what you want to. They are nothing more than that. God is doing the mirror image of what the soul is doing. God is manifesting souls to conduct explorations just like the soul is generating incarnations to conduct explorations. It is the exact same process. Not everything becomes a soul and not everything becomes an incarnation; there are other things and ways to explore.

Let's say you have a thousand incarnations; it's actually more than that. The soul puts all the pieces of all these explorations together and creates an understanding from them. God is fully aware of this process and what is learned by each soul. Just like individual souls put the learnings from all the incarnations together to create an understanding, God puts all the explorations from the innumerable souls together. It's just one process. I as an individual can have an individual sense of myself and not realize I'm really a soul. Eventually this misunderstanding dissolves and only the soul is left. The incarnation and all that was learned as well as the other incarnations and all they learned are in the soul. That also happens when the souls dissolve back into the Creator; it's the exact same process.

JOHANNA: So the experiences that the souls have that don't become incarnations are still experiences.

JOE: Exactly, they are explorations of the soul, and only some of them are incarnations. The soul is fully conscious of all the explorations of all the incarnations. The relationship between the incarnation and the soul is the same as between the soul and the Creator. Sometime after all the incarnations dissolve back into the soul and the soul is in its pure state, it will dissolve back into the Creator. That's how we are all one because in truth, there is nothing but the Creator exploring.

JOHANNA: Correct.

JOE: There is no consciousness other than the Creator's. There isn't an individual consciousness other than that. Part of the play of consciousness is that the various souls interact with one another and their incarnations interact with one another. Some of the explorations of the soul are like being part of a theatrical production in which the characters don't have the whole story. Other souls join the play because it's interesting and entertaining. It derives from a thought of God: what happens if I play out a little bit of amnesia to see what it looks like? It is not quite like that of course, but essentially, we're here for the experiences and the explorations.

JOHANNA: Is that where ego comes in, and is that to create a more individual experience?

JOE: In order for the incarnations that do not know they are actually God to function, they need an alternative belief system. The ego provides a structure that causes them to believe they are separate individuals. It happens to be incorrect, but it does allow them to function in this world.

JOHANNA: It feels like the collective heart consciousness that we tapped into on Saturday is the beginning of our journey across that bridge into Creator consciousness and the understanding that you just shared.

JOE: I think that level is when the incarnation has a much deeper understanding of the soul. There is also a greater two-way flow and less is masked. It is sometimes called the veil being removed. It is less ego identification and more soul identification.

JOHANNA: Correct.

JOE: The endgame for the series of incarnations is when you're so fully soul-conscious that you realize the ego is just an exploration, and that your incarnation was just an exploration. In the East, it is called enlightenment. You continue to play out the incarnation because you still have to walk around, but you realize this is nothing more than an exploration of the soul, and that everything around you is part of the exploration. It sometimes interacts with the explorations of other souls, so there's kind of a cosmic play going on. All of that funnels back up to the Creator. It is like a hologram; every layer is just a manifestation of the central layer but in a slightly different form. It is all interesting.

JOHANNA: Without all of the combined layers, the picture isn't complete.

JOE: What it boils down to is there is no need to do anything other than the exploration; that's all there is to do, whatever that is and wherever that takes you.

JOHANNA: And being aware of it.

JOE: And being aware of it, or not.

JOHANNA: That's true.

JOE: Exploring whether or not to be aware could be part of the exploration.

JOHANNA: Sometimes we are aware and sometimes we are not, it is all choice.

JOE: One of the possibilities in the exploration is to be conscious and fully aware of the play of consciousness while we are in the incarnation. That is known as self-realization or enlightenment. It pleases the Creator when an incarnation reaches that state, although "pleases" is not exactly correct because there is nothing that displeases, and there is no value of higher or lower. There is something to it that is just a little bit different than most of the incarnations because there are typically few times for each soul when it is in the incarnation and aware of the play of consciousness.

AN EXAMPLE OF THE ENERGY OF CRYSTALS

Sage, 4-4-19

This excerpt is from a reading Sage gave in Joe's study on a lovely quartz crystal with multiple points. Joe had purchased it in Arkansas a month before. One way to think about crystals is to conceptualize the universe as being created from conscious light that lowered its vibrational frequency to become other energies and matter. In this framework, crystals can be considered to be a nearly pure form of solidified light. As such, they have consciousness, energy and a strong connection to the Creator.

❖

SAGE: This is flower quartz, which means it is a healing stone.

JOE: It is from Mount Ida in Arkansas.

SAGE: It said its purpose was to remind you of the essence of your soul, of whom you are and who you were before you ever came into life. It was created in a very sacred place, and not only does it work as a healing stone, it also reminds you of the many different dimensions within the world, within the universe and within life. It says there is energy and beauty in this dimension, but that energy and beauty always extends far beyond what you are able to see. You need to start looking for that and allow your flow to go in that unseen direction. This stone also connects with the Arcturians, a master healing race who live in the Belt of Orion.

It says there have been energy pyramids set up in this room, and it

Mt. Ida flower quartz

is setting up another one. The energy at first is going downwards, and then it is slowly moving upwards. The energy line that is being created is yellow, which means it is a spiritual line.

The stone is also bringing in and anchoring feminine energy. It is doing the same with masculine energy, but to a lesser extent. The feminine energy is coming in very strong while the masculine energy is coming in very softly, and there is not as much of it. The stone said the earth needs the feminine energy to be the predominant now because that energy doesn't go to the energy of war and chaos as quickly as masculine energy will.

The stone is multidimensional; it was blessed as it was formed, and it was blessed again after it came out of the Earth. It says it stands alone and wants to be placed on a shelf by itself.

YOU HAVE TO FEED THE DRAGONS EVERY DAY

The Healing Light Group, 4-13-19

JOE: I recently received a message from Spirit about the five origami dragons that my grandson made that are in my study. They're all in a little group on a high shelf. The message was, you have to feed the dragons every day. It doesn't say what they eat, but I have to figure that out and feed them every day.

H.M.: I think you need to feed them with attention.

JOE: That is what we do, so Tucker and I feed the dragons every day.

SAGE: You can see they are paper, but they have a seeming realness to them. One time when Joe and I were working in that room, we noticed the largest of the dragons had an almost palpable energy. We could just feel it emanating energy. Just at that moment, Tucker walks in and growls at the dragon [group laughter].

JOE: That dragon had been on my shelf for several years, and Tucker has never previously growled at it. He must have somehow pick up on that same energy Sage and I were feeling.

The origami black dragon

THE ROLE OF THE LIGHTWORKERS

Johanna, 4-23-19

T*his took place during a healing session for Joe.*

❖

JOE: So this may well be the beginning of an eleven-year cycle. My retirement is in two months, and the trip to Sedona, Santa Fe, and Arkansas that I just came back from might all have been a part of setting it up.

JOHANNA: Right, the big shifting. I am getting that you are supposed to hold this (the blue flash crystal Joe bought in Arkansas) over your lung while I hold these other stones.

JOE: I feel something. I am getting the message that the troubles in my lungs are not something I did wrong that I have to deal with, but rather is something that I offered to carry so that it could be transformed.

JOHANNA: Yes, it feels like that transformation is going on now. It's laying some groundwork, like a foundation.

JOE: I can feel that this stone is directing pure divine energy to where it needs to go in my lung, like a wand or something. It is going right to what you might consider the darkness in my lungs. So it is not going to me as Joe; it is going to whatever I have been carrying, and it is transforming it into something else.

JOHANNA: Correct. It feels like it is not just related to the symptoms you have, but is more related to grief. It is like you're releasing grief for the universe.

JOE: Grief for the whole universe [humorously]? Why not?

JOHANNA: In your spare time [jokingly]. I am feeling like each of us in the Healing Light Group is carrying something.

JOE: I can feel my lung heating up on the inside.

JOE: There are other places in this world and other beings doing the same kind of work that we are doing.

JOHANNA: I was just going to say that it feels like we're in a pod that is connected around the globe and through the universe that is doing the same stuff.

JOE: We are contributing a piece to that much larger work. It is connecting to the aspect of grief from what you might call the fall of humanity, which is not quite the right name. It was when humanity went so deep into this density that it lost contact with the divine. That caused enormous pain, and there is huge grief connected with it. That larger effort is working on releasing that grief.

JOHANNA: It feels like the energy is doing a cross section of your lung from top to bottom. It is slicing down through and opening it up so they can scoop out what they are putting in air quotes as "rotten."

JOE: I am getting the understanding that because this pain in humankind is held in the third dimension, it is helpful for Lightworkers to carry it in our own bodies in the third dimension so the etheric beings working to remove this pain have the correct frequencies to clear it. Having a carrier in this dimension assisting them allows for more precise work. I have often thought of myself like a paratrooper behind enemy lines who guides the missiles and airstrikes. It is kind of a violent metaphor, but it's the person on the ground who can direct the missiles to pinpoint accuracy. At the same time, it's important for the stones, for you, and the other beings doing this healing work to be in the third dimension as well. Once again, it allows for greater precision of the energies to work.

JOHANNA: Correct. It also gives awareness of what's possible and what's being done. It allows people to have more hope for the future. Without that, people will just think that the pain is going to remain.

JOE: It's more than pain; it's the scarring as well. The scarring is an additional limitation that came from dealing with the pain for so long. There are other people involved in this work. They are telling me that everyone in the Healing Light Group is a carrier.

JOHANNA: It feels like they are removing all of the memory of that pain from you. I think the purpose of the blue flash crystal is also to meet the frequency of your crystalline body and do some work on it.

JOE: I am hearing that this was orchestrated so long ago that we would have trouble comprehending how long ago this was planned. Think when the stone was created with this project in mind. How long ago was that? That's when the plan was made.

JOHANNA: It's a good thing they are patient [laughter].

WE ARE THE WORLD

Sage and Johanna, 4-27-19

T*his took place following a healing session for Joe.*

❖

SAGE: How do you feel?

JOE: Wonderful.

SAGE: Well, those outside of us did a lot of work.

JOE: Thank you both and everyone else. This seems a little bit odd, but clearing me has to do with clearing the world.

SAGE AND JOHANNA: Yes.

JOE: I do not know all the pieces, but I am connected in some way with clearing the world.

JOHANNA: That is because we are the world. We are God. Clearing us clears everything out. We need to start seeing ourselves not just as individuals in a body but as whole beings connected to all other beings.

THE ENERGY OF RELEASE

Johanna, 6-26-19

This took place during a healing session for Joe.

❖

JOHANNA: We come from God almost like down a thread into our incarnation. Along that thread are different lifetimes and different dimensions. I have been working for the last couple of weeks with people on visualizing their thread. It's been interesting because most people's threads come down and goes right into their heart chakra. I usually see clumps of energy along that thread that seem to be stuck. Some of it is past lives and some of it is different dimensions. Just giving it attention, almost like shining a flashlight on it, seems to help the clumps disintegrate and release.

JOE: I like that thread idea and energy blockages on it.

JOHANNA: I don't know if it depicts karma or past issues, but just giving it attention allows it to soften and dissipate.

JOE: When you looked at me, did you see evidence on my thread about my connection with some pretty bad groups in the past?

JOHANNA: I saw some heaviness, nothing more than that.

JOE: Sage said I had a few lifetimes in which I connected with a satanic or some other group that was truly terrible. One thing I learned from those negative lifetimes was that you could not look directly at that kind of evil because that would cause you to connect with it. Once connected, you couldn't disconnect. It is like the story of Perseus and Medusa in which she is so ugly (read evil) that anyone who looked directly at her would turn to stone. That piece of knowledge is important and was hard-gained.

This connects with the energy of release that Sage and I have been working with. Those negative groups do not like the energies of light and love. If you send those energies, they just cringe. On the other hand, if you send them the energy of release, they appreciate it. Light and love is not for everybody at this time. I am trying to figure out what my work is at this point and where that leaves me regarding the energy of release. What I came up with was breathing in light and love and breathing out release. I'm not sure that is optimal, however. Also, I can't send directly to negative groups because I don't want to get caught in their negative energy. So how does this all work now?

JOHANNA: To me, it feels like you put release on a tray of light and love. You are not going to get them to take the light and love, but if you just send release, I am not sure it will get to where it needs to go. It's almost like diluting the light and love light with a bit of release. You can also try breathing in light and love with the intention of collecting whatever it is that needs to be released so that the release can happen with the exhale.

JOE: Okay, that probably has to happen at the cosmic heart level. I don't think at this point that I would do anything with my own energies, certainly not at that level.

The healing session begins.

I always feel good when I finish here. I think the session strengthened my connection with the cosmic heart. Part of that is knowing not to work with the energy of release unless it is through the cosmic heart.

JOHANNA: I felt Metatron come in, and he gave us information that we will be able to access about moving forward with the energy of release, but was also very clear that we are not the ones doing the release.

JOE: That is right. I have a little stuff of my own that is releasing, but that is minor.

JOHANNA: For us, I heard ambassadors for release. I think it is about teaching people how to release their stuff, but it is not us clearing it for them. They have to do the work. What I saw was a penny sitting on a counter and even if their action is just pushing that penny a little bit, that is them participating. So it could be them doing a lot or just little, but they are responsible for their own releasing. We can work with them on that, but it really feels like we're supposed to be moving forward with teaching people how to release and that it is okay to release. Some people are not sure who they would be without that history. It needs to be communicated that you are still the divine being that you were created to be.

EFFORT IS NOT NEEDED

Johanna, 7-6-19

THIS TOOK PLACE *following a healing session for Joe.*

❖

JOHANNA: What I felt about 10 minutes ago was kind of an unveiling of who you are. You're not meant to play small anymore. Who you truly are, your essence, your being, everything beyond your human form was just brought forth. When I worked on your head, there was this burst of energy and I saw bright white. It was just an overwhelming kind of peaceful---just emergence. It felt familiar, like it was your energy; it was just not kept in this human restriction.

JOE: I felt a flooding in of light that was very pleasant. I thought I could happily just stay here forever doing this, and then I became happy. I haven't been happy for a long time.

JOHANNA: It felt like everything finally aligned and then erupted into your essence, and your soul spilled out. Obviously your physical body is still here, but it's not restricting anything anymore. When you first lay down and I said you were working on me more than I was working on you, it was because I felt an energy coming from you that literally went into my heart and started pulling stuff out. It was pulling and pulling to the point where it felt like I had a brick in me trying to come out through a needle hole. It eventually came through, and it felt like we were partners.

JOE: Yes, I felt that connection too, and then it expanded beyond just the two of us to the whole group.

JOHANNA: Yes, it feels like we just stepped into a whole new realm of possibilities, not responsibilities. It is more up to us to choose what we want to do and where to take it from here.

JOE: Yes, and it won't be work. It will be just being and doing what we choose to do.

JOHANNA: Now I feel a sphere around you and one around me and one around this building.

JOE: I very much was feeling the energy around us. I think that was because of the nature of the work we did as a group. We created and facilitated a kind of an energy that does not need us to continue.

JOHANNA: We have rubbed the lamp and the genie is now out. We are supposed to enjoy each other more now, and be working from a space of joy.

JOE: We don't need to put effort into that. Effort is not needed anymore. It's just following the energies, and the energies are joyful happy energies. They're not energies that call for great effort. It doesn't mean we will not dig a ditch sometime, but it will be because it's in line with what we want to do.

ASK FOR ASSISTANCE

Sage and Johanna, 9-3-19

T*his took place during a healing session for Joe.*

❖

JOE: I have a few more tests to run in the next couple of days with my pulmonologist. He says my lungs are damaged, but that is not causing my shortness of breath and fatigue. My cardiologist says my heart is damaged, but that is also not causing my current problems. The pulmonologist says we don't really know what your problem is, but it is clear something is not working the way it should. He wants to check to see if it is vocal cord dysfunction or sleep apnea.

JOHANNA: I have a third possibility; maybe you're traveling through dimensions, and you are not needing to use the same physiology in those other dimensions. It is just getting you screwed up.

JOE: [laughing) Okay, I will mention that to my pulmonologist and see if he can run that one down also. [All laughing]

SAGE: I am being told to tell you that when you go into meditation, you need to set up parameters that all energy coming in will be beneficial to your health and that the energies are in alignment with your body's energies. You need to let them know that you are willing to be of service, but to do that, your body needs to be at your highest. So ask them to do that for you.

JOE: Sounds good.

SAGE: He is showing you meditating, and he says you are too trusting. You just figure whatever you need will happen. Because you are going into higher energies now, you need to set up for them that this is a human body and that the energies are different. Everything needs to be in alignment with a human body. Nothing is ever done negatively, but you need to set up those parameters so it will be easier for you. Also, you need to be very, very grounded.

Do you have any particular Beings you ask to help you?

JOE: I very seldom directly ask for help for me, but I do connect with Mother Mary, Mary Magdalene, Jesus and Lightest on a regular basis. It is almost as if we work together as a team.

SAGE: He says why don't you ask for things for yourself?

JOE: I didn't know it worked that way. I just try to be of service.

SAGE: Nope. He said to do your highest work, you need to be at your highest, so ask for help. He says to ask Jesus to go in and work on your body before you start to work.

JOHANNA: A message came in that said even though we vibrate at a higher level, we still need to recognize we are human and ask for help when we need it. Ask for the healing, for assistance, for strength, for perseverance, whatever. Even though we have moved up somewhat, that does not mean we are independent. In fact, we may need more of their help as we make these transitions. It is like when you climb a mountain, the air gets thinner and you need more assistance as you get higher.

MEDIEVAL TIMES AND A DRAGON COMPANION

Carylanne Part 1, 3-4-20

T<small>HIS IS THE</small> *first of two excerpts from a psychic reading Joe received.*

❖

C<small>ARYLANNE</small>: We welcome the Christ, Joe's guides, and the archangels Michael, Gabriel, Raphael and Uriel to stand around the four directions of our energy fields. We honor Earth Mother and Father Sky and all of life. And so it is. So Joe, what is the first area that you're interested in hearing about?

J<small>OE</small>: I don't have an area. Whatever you think is appropriate for me to know is fine. It can be guidance, information, healing or whatever comes up.

C<small>ARYLANNE</small>: I am seeing a stone path, and you have been on this stone path before. It looks like medieval times, and there was a lot of unrest. You carried a sword and a shield because there was much to slay. You were in service to a high priestess and learned the Way of the Goddess in this incarnation. I'm also seeing a dragon that is literally walking with you like a pal. He says he is your way-shower and the part of you that knows the great one.

Over on the right, I am seeing a temple-like room. There is a guardian over your left shoulder with a staff. He has been with you since you were three years old in this lifetime. He is a very wise and ancient one. They are showing me different pictures.

There is a cup that some would consider to be the "Cup" that Jesus drank from. It seems as though these pieces are being shown to you, not only to direct you on your path, but to let you know that you are coming to some type of a culmination of understanding. It's like you are gathering all these pieces of yourself and coming into wholeness. Do you see?

JOE: I believe that is correct.

CARYLANNE: This is interesting. Did you do some type of work with children? The spiritual information that you give to these children is very important. They are very eager to learn. The children represent the playfulness. The children represent the innocence. It's not about this being all serious. It's about the joy of life.

CARYLANNE: You seem to keep climbing up this ladder of spiritual knowledge and then you get to a certain point and you say ok, and they are like, "No, no, keep going! It's time; it's time to come up!" There is a piece that has to do with surrender. It is time to transmute any limitations that keep you held back in any way. This will be a big part of the next ten years. Your presence on the planet is a presence of light, peace, compassion and serenity. It is needed.

WORKING WITH THE TRANSITION

Carylanne Part 2, 3-4-20

JOE: I have been working to assist with the transition (see the Notes Section) almost since the transition was planned. I am part of a large group of beings (the Lightworkers) that has been working for eons to bring light and love to that section of humanity that had blocked the divine light so much that they could no longer perceive it. They are led by Lord Sananda (Jesus), and the plan was to incarnate here and bring them light from the inside because they had almost totally blocked the external light.

CARYLANNE: You know that?

JOE: Yes. I came to this planet to work with the transition. I was, relatively speaking compared to most of the inhabitants here, a higher vibrational being. I went through the incarnation cycle on Earth like the other beings on this planet instead of working from the outside like an archangel. The state of human kind was such that just energies alone from the outside, no matter how wonderful, were insufficient to create the transition. I worked from the inside as a human who went through the process of multiple incarnations.

CARYLANNE: It seems that you had many incarnations where you had access to the great teachings way before others. Because of this access, you are an integral part of the ascension that is happening on the planet. Have you written about any of this?

JOE: No.

CARYLANNE: Would you?

JOE: Why do you ask? Oh, they're asking me. I thought you were asking me.

CARYLANNE: They're saying, "Would you?"

JOE: Well, I am not going to say no [laughter].

CARYLANNE: It seems that there is information that needs to come out and that you have the information. They're asking you to gather the information, and share it because other people need to know. Other people need to know that what they know is true.

RECYCLING THE ENERGY OF PAIN AND FEAR

Sage and Johanna Part 1, 8-11-21

This is the *first of four excerpts prior to a healing session for Joe.*

❖

SAGE: You are a being of light that knows and believes at a level beyond most humans. As this being, you can identify and help reduce the negativity that massive numbers of people are spewing out into the world. Look at it like you see the negativity coming, and you are assisting it to turn the corner and be recycled. It comes, and you help it to be recycled. Directing the flow to be recycled allows that massive pile of energy to come back to those people and comfort them. They are so raw and afraid that they have great struggles throughout their life. They are, on an unconscious level, searching for a way out of their pain.

By recycling, that energy can then come back to them, and they can find more peace. There are many Lightworkers who could do this, but few choose to because they don't know the process. As you assist with the recycling, somehow others are tapping in and they can then do the process for other people. Fear stops some of the Lightworkers because they are afraid of what that might mean for them. They must process through their own fear before they can even consider doing this work.

HIGHER LEVEL ENERGY

Sage and Johanna Part 2, 8-11-21

SAGE: THERE are Lightworkers working at a level that normally Lightworkers do not touch into. Because of their commitment, responsibility and their willingness to go to the highest vibration without fear, they are going to a much higher level. It's like being at level eight going to a twenty with just a snap of your fingers.

There are universal beings from out just before the Milky Way coming in. They are very high vibrational level beings and their path is to assist the higher level Lightworkers. They ask that we pay attention to their energy and allow ourselves to be a clear vehicle for it. They also want us to ask them what, if anything, we need to do. Many times we will not need to do anything. He is showing me that as they come into our universe, they're adjusting their energy and slowly bringing it down into our bodies. As they do that, we radiate a pure white light that is a very high intensity. It just goes out and encompasses everything. We do not need to do anything accept allow them to work through us. That light is within our bodies, and we can ask it to assist with whatever is going on. The universal beings can direct it to wherever we want it to go. They know our value because there are not many yet who can tolerate that intensity. They're doing Namaste as the energy moves off.

He says, "Know that you are blessed even though it does not feel like it as you go through your human challenges. You are amazing individuals that make it possible for us to come and work within this realm." When I feel them, they're very warm, comforting, and just incredible. They bring with them a very high radiance, light and energy. That's funny, someone just said, "And we know where you live" [laughter from Joe and Sage].

JOE: They have a sense of humor obviously.

SAGE: I am finding that more and more. They're radiating great gratitude because he says, "You don't know what you are doing. You really don't know what you're doing. You do not know the good that you do just by being who you are and being able to receive this energy." He says the energy goes to people and they are changed, but they may know it at the time. Whenever they are ready, they will suddenly be able to do things and let go of things that they didn't think they could do before.

JOE: It sounds like the energy enters their fields, and it is available to them when they're ready.

SAGE: Yes. He said it is simply a matter of our holding that energy, and it just goes out to thousands.

There's a Native American influence coming in, and I hear Native American drums. They are calling to the wise ones and their ancestors to be present, and also for people all over to just to be present for the here and now. It's like there are two drums; one is calling everybody, and right behind it is a second drum. It is calling Lightworkers to stand up and come forward. They have to do both drums because the population needs so much healing.

When they call the Lightworkers with the second drum, I see people just all of a sudden come awake and stand up. There are not a lot of them, just one every once in a while. It is like they are suddenly wide awake and looking around. That couldn't have happen if earlier Lightworkers had not assisted with bringing in and holding higher energies for many decades because the energies needed to be stable before the newer Lightworkers could be called. Otherwise, it would have been too much for them. They will be assisted to understand the process.

We need to give thanks for the spiritual and energy work the universal beings do with us because that gratitude strengthens us and makes a stronger connection. He says that energy brings new knowledge. You are to start your journey; you are your light; you are God that resides within; you are the seed; it is time to grow.

Short Pause

SAGE: When you start tuning in to the deeper levels, it's like you're gone and you're not energetically flowing. They said you need to be a little bit more a part of the process, and feel the energy instead of just saying ok and drifting off. You need to be in both modes; the here and the there.

JOE: So basically, be more engaged in it as opposed to just setting it up and letting it run itself.

JOHANNA: I feel like we are supposed to be stepping out beyond what we ever thought we could be and really acknowledging our connection with the universe. We are all in this together, and for us to limit ourselves to even the fact that we have energy just in the US is ridiculous and even more ridiculous to think it is just in our state or city. They are showing me it is like taking off the top of the head and just allowing ourselves to leave our brain, to leave it behind and just feel. It really is about expanding everything we can be in order to step into the energy that is coming. Otherwise, it will just plow us over, and we will be stuck in the mud.

JOE: So they want us to be functional with the new energies, not just blotto.

JOHANNA: Right. It is like when we first started the Healing Light Group and they asked us to allow them to use us. That was like a minuscule drop in the bucket compared to what is expected of us now. Now we are supposed to be like these huge bits of energy, and it's not just us individually, or collectively, or the healing group; its humanity. Humanity has to get on the same page of being able to receive and also allow. We don't have to do anything; we don't have to send anything; we just need to allow and be within that energy. That's about it.

SAGE: Yes. Don't just go off; make sure you're still here and engaged.

JOHANNA: I am feeling they have transmuted much of our energy and much of our being from third-dimensional human into fifth-dimensional crystalline. I think the activations that have taken place over the past years have started to flip the switch so that all of our energies are coming together.

SAGE: Yes. They keep saying that a call will go out, but people have to be willing.

JOE: Yes, even the Lightworkers have to be willing.

JOHANNA: Well, I think the Lightworkers have to be willing to make adjustments. You know it is like what I'm doing is completely different than what I did last time I worked on you. I am sure the same is true of Sage and anybody else here. I feel like I'm traveling through dimensions more frequently and being aware that I'm doing that. I don't think I really acknowledged that before.

SAGE: They are just saying it is time, it is time.

JOHANNA: It is beyond time.

SAGE: Yes, it is beyond time. He just wants to reiterate that we need to see everybody as they are today, so that they can move forward from this person today. We need to leave who they were in the past behind.

JOHANNA: That also includes us. We need to see ourselves as who we are today and not who we used to be. It is like this physical being that you see when you look in the mirror on the wall is completely different than the internal mirror that you need to look at. The internal mirror is the one that shows you who you are: your soul. That's the mirror we need to be reflecting on. Once we start changing our perception of ourselves, we will start changing the perception of other people around us and getting away from judgment.

THERE IS ONLY ONE KIND OF HEALING

Sage and Johanna Part 3, 8-11-21

JOE: They are telling me that there is only one kind of healing. All forms and all things that anyone thinks they are doing in terms of healing are only approximating that one kind of healing, which is simply removing the veil that keep a soul or incarnation from knowing who they really are. All healing amounts to removing the barriers to seeing and knowing who you are. Sometimes, the barriers are so thick and so dense, that you think you are working on a foot, or a heart, or a cognitive problem, or an illness, but you are only even thinking that because the barriers are so thick at that point. As the barriers thin, you realize all healing is simply removing those barriers. Removing them allows the pure light and love to enter the incarnation, and that brings about what people think of as healing.

JOHANNA: That's the best way I've ever heard it described.

JOE: They gave it to me to give it to you because that's what your new method is. You are working directly on removing or lessening of the barrier between the incarnation and the divine. That's the light and the energy that you are working with right now.

JOHANNA: I keep hearing stuff about the internal mirror. It feels like we have to look within.

JOE: That is so intense. I'm not used to looking in that mirror.

JOHANNA: Exactly.

JOE: Another way of phrasing "looking at the mirror" is to see through the barrier or to see without the barrier being present.

JOHANNA: Most people don't understand that. They understand a mirror.

JOE: Barrier maybe the wrong word. Veil is a little bit more accurate. When the veil is really strong and dense, it is like a barrier. But at the higher frequencies, it is more of a veil that you have at least some understanding of what's on the other side. It is more like taking a veil that is translucent and making it transparent, and then eventually removing it completely.

JOHANNA: I was given the idea of the mirror because it is something we have to do ourselves. We can seek healing from other people, but it's not going to be complete until we do it ourselves. It is about receiving and integrating any healing, and it is dependent upon knowing that we can be healed and are worthy of being healed.

THE VIBRATION OF CREATION

Sage and Johanna Part 4, 8-11-21

JOE: I am receiving a musical metaphor. We can think of each of us individually as a note and know our souls often work together and combine our three notes into a chord. That's essentially what the three of us are doing here. The universal beings are coming in and adding orchestration to that chord, which expands the sound in that metaphor to a fuller sound. It has more nuances and harmonics than you can get from a single note or a single chord. That orchestration includes connecting us at a greater level with other Lightworkers past and present. So the chord that sounds then, actually it is not just a chord but is now music. That music resembles the sounds of the divine when the universe was created. You can think of it as OM, but it is not exactly OM. So we are approximating that original sound through the work of our souls, the other Lightworkers, and the universal beings. That is what is happening here. That sound has the frequency and the power to effect great change. It is part of the energy behind the ascension that is ongoing now. In the metaphor of the music, the Creator is the conductor.

JOHANNA: I heard it is the vibration of creation.

JOE: The vibration of creation; that's the sound it is approximating. The original wave of the creation of this universe was Om Namah Shivaya, and this is a variation of that. It is a new creation built upon the old one. That's one of the reasons we can't think of ourselves as small; we have to understand that we are notes within that new wave of creation. That vibration of creation is sweeping through at least this galaxy, maybe even further. We are part of that orchestration, and once that happens, you're no longer just an individual note. We are part of the orchestration of the larger whole, and that is how we should understand ourselves.

Once we let go of our ego, our desires and our thoughts manifest in the appropriate timeframe because we are an aspect of that wave of creation. It is manifesting the thoughts and desires that bubble up within that wave, which come from the elements within the wave. That is how flow happens. It's automatic when you're in that vibration. When you're aware that you are in it, when you accept that you are part of it, and transcend the ego, then you are part of the creative process for what happens.

When I was in my 20s, I saw and felt the vibrational wave that was Om Namah Shivaya. It was an immensely powerful vibration that was moving across my visual horizon while I was in a vision state, and it created the universe as it rolled forward. It was the creative vibration of our universe. You can think that in front of it was nothing, and it was rolling across the vast empty space and leaving behind the universe. The part of us that has transcended ego is part of that new wave, although at that point, it is not us as individuals. This is not an offshoot of that prior Om Namah Shivaya, it is an…

JOHANNA: Extension.

JOE: Extension might be a good way to put it. It's new in itself, but it's related to Om Namah Shivaya, even though it is separate.

SAGE: It is the base. Om Namah Shivaya is the base from which a new vibration has been created.

JOE: Ok, that makes sense. It is manifesting as that vibration rolls forward. Now it is rolling through an existing universe, and it is in our galaxy creating the ascension that is affecting the galaxy. That is the difference; I believe that Om Namah Shivaya rolled through emptiness. This new wave is rolling through the existing universe, or at least this portion of the universe.

SAGE: As you talk about it, I feel such incredible warmth and love that is part of it.

JOE: Ok. This ties in from 15 minutes ago with the healing that Johanna is working with. In effect, what that new vibrational wave is doing is taking away the veils between what was the existing universe and the divine. It is rolling through and removing the veils, not 100%, but it is turning them much more translucent/transparent depending on what it encounters. It is taking them to the next level of transparency.

JOHANNA: I feel it is also laying down a new method of communication that we are going to have to adapt to or utilize to assist with the veil being lifted.

JOE: Ok.

JOHANNA: I get a strong sense of throat stuff and communication. It just feels like there is going to be a different or an enhanced way of communicating. I'm seeing something, and the words that are coming to me are "debris field." It feels like as the new wave comes through, some of the stuff from the old wave is being released, and we need to at least acknowledge that it is being released. It needs to be returned to neutral energy so that it can be used again.

PART 2:
LIVING IN THE LIGHT

ABOUT THIS SECTION

As the spiritual aspect of my life has developed, there is a flow which decreases the separation between the internal and external worlds, between thoughts and manifestation, between the personal and the cosmic. In this section, I provide some examples from my own life of what I term as fourth-dimensional experiences where life has less resistance and greater harmonious flow. These are the moments when the universe conspires to help you and when you feel the beauty and divinity which underlies this reality. They are in keeping with my belief that I have clear but unseen direction and guidance from what appears to be a divine source regarding energy and healing, to move in the direction of ego diminishment, and to embody light and love.

STRONG INTUITION PREVENTS POSSIBLE PARALYSIS

October, 1978

JOE: I had a wonderful radiation oncologist, Dr. S, treat me for my Stage III Hodgkin's Disease. He told me that I was going to need thirty to thirty-five radiation treatments to my chest immediately because I had a large fast-growing tumor over my heart. Then they would remove my spleen and do another sixty radiation treatments from the lower chest to the groin. The treatments started right away. They had drawn a treatment map on my body with a marker to mark the special points that the beams had to hit, and I was told not to wash my chest until the radiation there was completed.

LAURA: I would go with Joe to radiation on Wednesdays, which was the day he saw Dr. S each week for a consult. Now on this Wednesday, they talked for a long time. They had a very warm relationship and you could just tell that Dr. S had taken us under his wing because we were young newlyweds. Joe explained why he thought he had already had a tolerance dose of radiation to the chest and therefore did not want to take the remaining few scheduled treatments for that area. Considering this, Dr. S expressed understanding and concern and said that he wanted to take a look.

JOE: I should probably interject that before we went in that morning, I had a strong intuitive sense that I had enough radiation to the chest. I had at that point, perhaps thirty-one or thirty-two treatments and I was scheduled for thirty-five. I just knew I had enough. I was still going to do the rest of the treatments to the two other parts of my body, but I knew that I was done with the torso. So I erased the marks on my chest that were used to line up the radiation machine for treatment.

LAURA: Joe took his shirt off and when Dr. S l saw that there were no more lines, he just came unglued and was absolutely furious saying, "God damn you, Joe! When are you ever going to accept that you are the patient and I am the doctor!" But Joe is always unflappable, never confrontational, and his doctor had to accept it.

As it turned out, about two months later, Joe started to have electrical jolts in his spine when he bent his head forward. Dr. S was stunned with this news and said it was caused by the breaking down of the myelin sheath which protects the nerves in the spinal column. It was a rare side effect of cervical radiation and directly related to the dose of radiation received. He was baffled with how Joe knew to stop the treatments when he did, because had he continued with those few additional treatments, there was a good chance of him being permanently paralyzed.

SAVED WITH A ROLL OF PAPER TOWELS

March, 1989

I HAD BEEN suffering with what looked like a recurrence of my Hodgkin's disease in my lungs for several years when my doctor convinced me to undergo lung surgery in March of 1989. The plan was to get a definitive diagnosis and remove the right lower lobe that had looked problematic on the CAT scan if cancer was confirmed. I had previously undergone two needle biopsies and two bronchoscopies, but none procured enough of the problematic tissue in my lung for a diagnosis. The surgery confirmed that I had Stage IV Hodgkin's disease, but two serious unexpected problems occurred.

❖

The first was that I had cancer in all five lobes, not just the lower right. The surgeon made the decision to sew me up without attempting to cut out the cancer, leaving me to rely on chemotherapy for my survival. The second problem was that, unbeknownst to anyone, my decade-long fight with cancer had left me malnourished, resulting in my eight-inch incision not healing properly, which in turn resulted in the incision bursting open a week after surgery. I had been discharged on Friday and was at home with Laura on Sunday morning just two days later when we notice the incision beginning to open and blood dripping from my side.

During the minutes after our frantic message to the surgeon and his return call, a seemingly finely- orchestrated divine intervention in the form of Laura's best friend occurred. Toni was an RN and was on her way to church when she decided to travel via our rural road and then also made the decision to stop in unannounced and see how we were doing after the surgery. Unbelievably, she arrived seconds after the wound had opened much wider and blood started gushing. I was in the kitchen sitting on a chair as we waited because I did not want the blood to ruin the carpets. Toni quickly grabbed a roll of paper towels from the counter and stuck it in the wound to control the bleeding. She held it under pressure until the ambulance came.

In hindsight, it seems like a simple life-saving act. But in the panic of the moment, I don't think either Laura or I would have thought of doing that. Thank you Toni.

In this world, anyone who does not believe in miracles is not a Realist.
— anonymous

We commissioned this piece of calligraphy modeled after one that was hanging in the oncology infusion center where Joe received chemotherapy.

FORTY-TO-ONE ODDS AGAINST GETTING IN TO GRADUATE SCHOOL

1994

JOE: I came out of my second bout of cancer with a strong interest in studying the psychological aspects of chemotherapy-related side effects, particularly the role of expectations. This came out of my own experiences. When I began chemotherapy, I was certain I would have terrible nausea and vomiting, and sure enough I did. I wrote this up as a possible research idea and was able to get an appointment to discuss it with a cancer researcher at our nearby university. He did not seem to mind that I was a carpenter at the time.

LAURA: This professor was Joe's future boss, Dr. M. They talked about Joe's research ideas and the work that interested Joe. Many years later, when Joe worked in the Cancer Center, Dr. M loved to tell the story of the carpenter with a tool belt who came to see him and discuss his research ideas. Their first encounter ended with him saying, "Mr. Roscoe, this is all very well and good, but you would need a PhD to do this work. So if you get your PhD, come back and see me."

JOE: So I applied to the Department of Psychology. When my first application was not successful, I went to talk to a professor in the Department and asked if there was anything I could do to increase my chances. He said we like you, but we don't do cancer research here. Why don't you go to Carnegie Mellon or some school where they do this work? But since our family lived here, I told him that this had to be the place for me. He explained that they typically get about forty applicants per year for their program and take only one. He said that my only chance would be if there was no one they liked the following year among all the applicants; then they might consider me. Since that was better than no chance, I applied again.

When by March I hadn't heard anything, I called him up, told him who I was and reminded him that he said they would consider me that if they didn't find a candidate they liked. Well, they had not accepted anyone, and he said he would find my application. After a long pause he said...

LAURA: "We forgot all about you, Joe."

JOE: He asked me to give him a minute and it sounded like he left the room to go somewhere while I was still on the phone. He came back and asked, "Can you come in tomorrow morning about 9:30? I've set up some interviews for you." So I did, and they took me. He said that we still don't do cancer research here, so we'll give you two years. We will teach you the basics, but for you to finish your PhD, you will have to find somebody who is able to teach you what you want to learn, and who is willing to become your professor and mentor for your dissertation.

LAURA: So the University made a commitment to teach Joe the first two years of Social Psychology, and it was up to him to find a mentor so that he could specialize in cancer side effect research. Fast forward two years: Joe was delivering a package to one of his teachers in the hospital and happened to walk past the office of Dr. M who said, "Hey, wait. You're that guy! You're that carpenter. What are you doing here?"

JOE: I said, "I'm getting my PhD as you suggested." He seemed incredulous and asked, "Right here?" "Yes," I said. "I didn't want to move." So he asked me to come and see him later that day. We sat down in the late afternoon and I told him that I had just finished my second year of grad school. He asked, "Do you want a job?" And I asked, "Will you be my mentor and professor, because I need a content specialist in the Cancer Center to finish my doctoral program?"

Doctor M agreed and took over that role. I received my PhD four years later with Dr. M as my dissertation advisor, and worked for him at the Cancer Center for 23 years.

HUMMINGBIRDS

8-25-11

I WAS WATCHING the hummingbirds just before sunset and noticed the incredible peace and harmony around me. I decided to send this peace and harmony with the assistance of one of my crystals to needed places in Africa. It felt very correct. A few minutes later, I noticed that the two hummingbirds, which had been fighting over the feeder in normal hummingbird fashion, were now drinking peacefully from the same feeder. In a moment, a third one and then a fourth one joined them, and there were four hummingbirds drinking from the same feeder, something we have never seen before or since. It lasted only a minute, just long enough for Laura to see, but not to get a good photograph.

8-28-18

Many years later, I was in my chair watching a hummingbird at the feeder and was trying to take a photo of it using my phone. Even though I spent about twenty minutes trying to do so, I was unable to get a good photo because the bird was in constant motion and moved to quickly for me.

At that point, I tried to communicate with it telepathically and let it know that I would be honored if it would let me take its picture, and could it help me out if it was ok with that. It might be just coincidence, but within the space of one minute, I was able to take several good photos. It was like the hummingbird was posing for me.

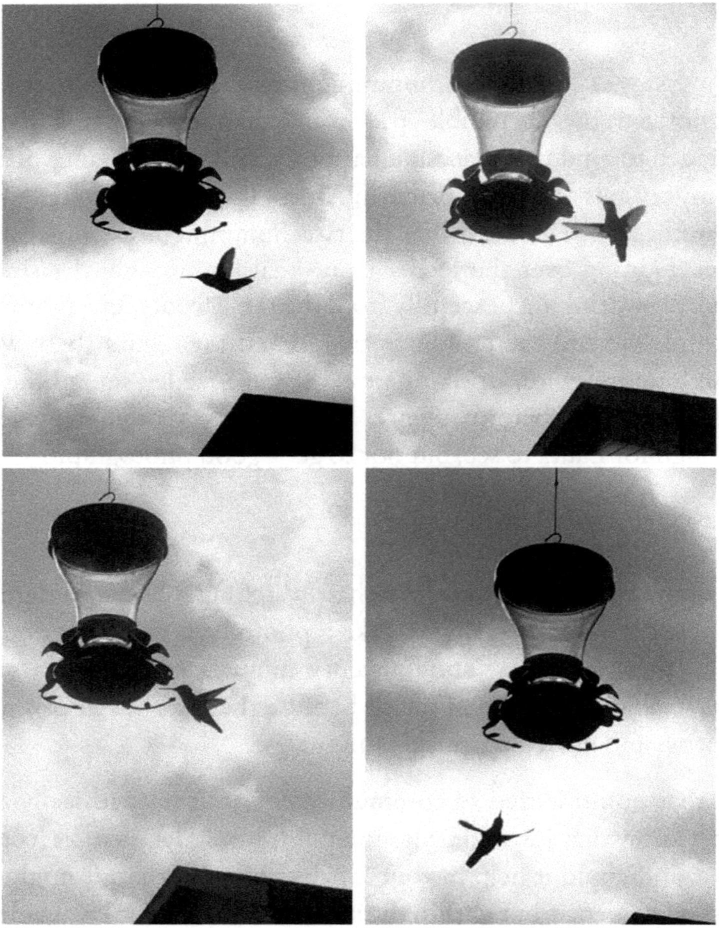

ROOSTER COMB MOUNTAIN

October, 2014

T*HIS ORCHESTRATION OF events by Spirit over a two-week period played out like a cosmic magic trick.*

❖

LAURA JOURNAL ENTRY ON OCTOBER 1, (EDITED): We are in Lake Placid for a two-week stay. This is definitely the place I love most in the world and I do not think I would ever tire of being here. But Joe still has four and a half years of work so is not ready to have a second home here. Despite this practical assessment, after visiting this area for the past fifteen years, Joe indulged me, and we went with a realtor to look at several places, with our favorite being a condo right on the shore of Lake Placid.

You Find the Path by Walking

LAURA JOURNAL ENTRY ON OCTOBER 5, (EDITED): The hike to Rooster Comb Mountain had been on our "future hike list" since 2009 when there was an article about it in the local paper. I had saved the article and each year I would enthusiastically bring it up as a possible hike. But each year Joe would find a reason to give it a no. He privately thought it would be too hard for him. The upper section of the trail goes over steep stone ledges which require scaling up wooden ladders to get to the summit. So, his caution was probably well-founded, as we later discovered. However, he decided that we would go this year on the following morning, which had the lowest chance of rain for the week.

LAURA JOURNAL ENTRY ON OCTOBER 6, (EDITED): We've both been a bit under the weather this trip and have a lot of lung congestion. I woke up at 9:00 a.m. after a difficult night's sleep and was lethargic and coughing. But, I remembered my own conviction about how to get through this particularly difficult and discouraging period of our previously happy life: "You find the path by walking." Just get up and get going. So I said nothing to Joe about feeling sick that morning. Instead, I took a hot shower and tried to eat a little toast for breakfast, which ended up making me sick. Not a very promising start.

I thought to myself, "If somehow I can actually do this hike while feeling so sick and if, against all odds we both actually make it up to the top, it will serve as a great lesson about the value perseverance in the face of adversity. I knew that I was going to have to dig deep to push through my fatigue and illness that day. I quietly contemplated how this could be a kind of new beginning.

The hike up Rooster Comb turned out to be one of the most wonderful ones we have ever done. It was an allegory which mirrored the difficulty and uncertainty of our life as well as our diminished hopes in the face of adversity. But it was not long before we received the first of three signs which appeared to us on this trail. The first was our totem, five geese together on a pond right at the beginning of the trail, which caused us to begin to take this journey very personally. The second sign was a yellow birch growing in a seemingly impossible way on top of a ten-foot-high boulder. As if that was not spectacular enough, it was illuminated by a most beautiful beam of sunlight even though we were deep in the woods,

We began our ascent that morning with a perfect autumn day. But two-thirds of the way to the top, a storm began to move in. Near the summit the wind picked up, the sky darkened and we could see it had moved directly over us on top of the mountain, which was the reason for the increasing wind and rain.

Fortunately, we had packed our large rain ponchos which were big enough to cover both body and backpack. They flapped in the strong wind as we ascended those wooden ladders, which were bolted into the vertical rock ledges near the top. At that point, I began to consider the wisdom of calling it a day. And I would have, but Joe wanted to keep going. By 2:30 pm we were on the summit, dispirited, hungry and bedraggled. The rain and wind had gotten even stronger so we sought cover in a thicket of trees a bit off the trail down from the summit where we hunkered down to stay as warm and dry as possible.

Once we accepted that we had to shelter in under the dense trees as best we could and simply wait, we decided to pull out the sandwiches we had packed. After a half hour or so, the storm began to move off the mountain and we were rewarded with the third sign we received that day: a spectacular view of a brilliant rainbow over the expansive valley below. We took it as a divine acknowledgement of our sadness and struggles as well as a message that we should persevere with the type of faith and effort it took to make the climb that day. We were filled with the sense that everything in our life was going to be alright... more than alright! This moment atop Rooster Comb turned out to be one of the great moments and great turning points of our married life.

Joe: I felt strong guidance to go on this hike even though I had been avoiding it for several years because of my diminished stamina. Even on the morning of the climb with Laura feeling sick, I received a message from Spirit to still go and received the same message when the storm hit while we were climbing. It was bewildering to Laura that I thought we should go on at those points because it was totally out of character for me. Once I saw the rainbow, I understood why this had all been arranged. It was a message to me that we needed to be in the Adirondacks for this next portion of our lives.

LATER NOTE FROM LAURA: We ended up buying that little condo on the shore of Lake Placid, with the mountain and lake views and hiking trails all around. The climb up Rooster Comb taught us to keep on dreaming and to keep on climbing. We spent a wonderful eight years living in Lake Placid as a second home. Joe was often able to work from there. During these years we climbed many more mountains and regained the sense that there were still adventures ahead for us.

TWO EXAMPLES OF FOURTH-DIMENSIONAL FLOW

August, 2020
(The Lawnmower)

One day when I was walking with Laura, I saw an unusual metal nut on the ground. Because I often pick up bits of trash on the street, I stuck it in my pocket. Some days later, I saw the maintenance man for our complex fiddling with a lawnmower. Apparently, an important nut had fallen off sometime earlier that made it impossible to operate it. I pulled out the nut, which was still in my pocket, and handed it to him. "Will this work?" I asked.

It obviously wasn't the missing nut, but it did have the correct thread and got the lawnmower working again.

(The Boogie Board)

In early August 2020, Laura had the idea that it would be fun to train our dog Tucker to ride on a mini surfboard/boogie board as a way of him playing in the water. Tucker loved to learn new tricks and loved being in the water, so it seemed like a natural. Laura went to every imaginable store in Lake Placid and none were available.

Unbelievably, our neighbor showed up at our door the next afternoon with a brand new boogie board still wrapped in the original cellophane. She had found it at a garage sale for five dollars that morning and thought Tucker and Laura might enjoy using it in the water together. Tucker loves it and is indeed riding it in the water.

TOPAZ

July, 2023

THE STORY STARTS when I was packing for our vacation in Blowing Rock, North Carolina. As I sometimes do, I asked if any of my crystals wanted to come with me. A small piece of topaz said it would like to go, so I stuck it in my pocket. About nine days later on our last full day in town, Laura and I were browsing in a vintage jewelry store, and she saw an amazing simple gold ring with a square cushion garnet that had a few tiny diamonds on either side. We both thought it looked beautiful, but she felt it was way beyond our budget, and she just walked away from it.

That ring and her love for it stuck in my mind, and I told her I wanted to stop at the store on our way home in the morning to look at it again. The website for the store said they opened at 11:00 and our checkout was at 10:00, so we decided to go out for breakfast at a café near the store.

This is when the universe stepped in to give us a boost. It started with my playing Wordle while waiting for our food. I knew after the second guess that the second letter was an O and the last was a Z, so I guessed TOPAZ, and that was the word. I then understood in a way that was quite powerful that something was happening outside of the dimension of regular living in relation to the ring. Laura was pretty resistant to spending that kind of money, and the fact that the store was closed when we got there even though it was ten after eleven confirmed her decision not to buy the ring.

I would've let it go at that if not for the word "topaz" coming up just thirty minutes earlier. So I persisted and went to the trouble of calling the online number for the store. Fortunately, the owner had provided her cell phone on her answering machine. I called and, amazingly, the owner answered. She was in her car about to leave town on an errand, but agreed to stop at her store on her way and meet us. Needless to say, we bought the ring and it is truly special. Laura just loves it. It turns out that the final piece of assistance from the universe was the fact that her website erroneously said she was open on Sunday at 11:00 even though she had not actually been open on a Sunday for over six months. We would never have even thought of going to the store Sunday or made the phone call if the website had not said the store would be open.

Laura says that she cannot properly put into words this meaning of this special garnet ring. Her original wedding ring was a very simple garnet in a bezel setting in a rose gold band that we asked a local artist to design and make. She feels there is definite meaning in being given a second beautiful garnet ring in the year of our forty-fifth wedding anniversary. We both feel a sense of understanding that we will probably not make it to our fiftieth anniversary, and this is why we were given this symbolic gift now at forty-five years. It feels like this will be our biggest milestone anniversary. So, we began our journey together with a garnet and we end our journey together with a garnet.

This felt to me like a powerful demonstration of fourth-dimensional living, where things flow between the worlds in a gentle and clear way. We are given insights and gifts and assistance. In this case, I feel a sense of knowingness that we are in the last part of our time together in this world. We are meant to treasure this special time.

PART 3: CLOSING THOUGHTS

WITH LOVE AND LIGHT

As I mentioned at the very beginning of this book, I was blessed as a young man with a mystical revelation that all is God. That revelation faded quickly, never to be replicated for me, but it left me with the clear understanding that my life's purpose would be to know, love and serve God. I find it more than a bit ironic that phrase came right out of the Baltimore Catechism I had been forced to study as a young Catholic and from a religion that I have not practiced for over fifty years. But if I apply my own understanding that God is everywhere, it follows that there is truth everywhere. It is just a matter of letting the aspect of truth that is most appropriate for you be the one that guides you at any given time.

Neither that divine revelation nor my newfound life purpose came with an instruction manual. Both left me with a host of questions, not the least of which was, what to do next? It was not at all clear to me what a life focused on knowing, loving and serving God would look like. I was pretty certain, also, that very few people would believe in or care about my new cosmic insight on the nature of God. I did not see a discernable path forward.

More than one poet has said that you find the path by walking, and that was certainly true for me. The answers came slowly over many decades: by reading, listening to teachers, from channeled guidance, by intuition, from dreams, from meditation, and by the people in my life and the work that I did. Often when I encountered a decision point or fork in the road, I relied on guidance, which I felt in the form of energy and then selected the path which resonated with the clearest energy. I was very fortunate that over the years and decades, important people, opportunities, experiences, and understandings came to me when I was ready for them.

I give marriage special mention because my path would have been immensely more difficult and likely not traversable without Laura. When I married Laura in 1978, I understood that marriage would be a vehicle for me to learn about love. I believe I even said something to that effect in my wedding vows thinking that was a lofty ideal, although I was clueless as to what that would actually mean in practice. The reality of learning about love is that it can only be learned through experience and years of walking the walk. Infatuation may have been a biological gift that helped us begin our forty-five-year journey together, but it was a mutual commitment to maintain a loving orientation toward one another that sustained us over the decades. It is through that commitment to her as well as hers to me that I learned most of what I know about love. In my twenties, one helpful understanding about being a couple while still maintaining our individual identities came to me: to be as close as two trees whose leaves touch when the wind blows.

I found that maintaining a loving orientation necessitated learning to love what she loved as much as I was able, whether or not it fit with my natural inclination. It also meant striving to be loving under all circumstances. It turns out that Laura has been my teacher for learning about love, just as I had envisioned on my wedding day. And in a very real way since everything is God, learning to love Laura for me was learning to love God.

The importance in my life of the friendship of fellow spiritual travelers cannot be over-emphasized. As I noted, it begins with my wife, who has been a companion for most of my life journey. She is also an energy healer. I have been truly blessed to find four great companions (Sage, Johanna, Judy and Mark); all were members of the Healing Light Group. They introduced me to aspects of God that I was unaware of time and time again, and also validated many of my own spiritual understandings and experiences. There is a synergy that develops in a group of spiritual seekers that allows for greater understanding than can be attained alone. This synergy became tangible when the entire Healing Light Group linked together through a conscious heart meditation that connected us to the cosmic heart. I believe that the cosmic heart is the heart of God and working with the group made it far more accessible and far easier to come to know God.

The soul understands fully that life in this dimension involves great suffering and pain and yet chooses to incarnate on Earth time and time again. The reason is that this world provides an opportunity and/or perhaps a school to learn to be more loving, and to be of service to God. There is so much need and suffering in this world that the opportunities to assist others and offer loving comfort are endless. For most of us, our souls sent us to this school to learn to be kind, to learn about love in its myriad forms and to learn to use power responsibly. It takes multiple lifetimes to fully master the curriculum.

I found the phrasing I came across in a book entitled, The Law of One to be a particularly helpful way to easily keep the above curriculum in mind. It is simply to move from an orientation of service to self to that of service to others. It fits perfectly with my understanding that God is everything and that one of my life's purposes is to serve God; service to others is therefore service to God.

One of my key understandings was that while at the level of the ego, we are surrounded by imperfection, viewed from a higher perspective, all is perfect, all is God. The understanding that all is God has enormous implications that conflict with what our ego believes. For example, if all is God, then we are God. If we are God and if God created this reality, then we created our own reality. If we created our own reality, then we are responsible for everything that happens to us. The human brain is largely incapable of making sense of these apparent paradoxes. But that is not the case for the heart, the mind, or the soul. I know from experience that the human heart has the ability to connect with the sea of divine love in which we are immersed. Similarly, the human mind has the ability to connect with the soul and understand that this seeming reality is just a play of consciousness and is not actually the true reality.

I have learned that letting go of actual or imagined injustices was a critical step in my spiritual growth because there are always grievances, and an attachment to them inhibits access to the higher vibrational levels. I also know growth is a process of expanding the sense of self and letting go of perceived limitations. At some point, this necessitates being aware that we are always connected to God. That can be either as Source or Creator directly, or if we prefer, to God as a named being such as Jesus or Mother Mary. I originally found the latter more relatable and approachable but now gravitate to Creator; it is our choice. We are also able to communicate with our soul, with angels and other higher dimensional beings that are always available for guidance. For me, the communication can comes in many different ways, e.g., through intuition, channeling and sometimes through unexpected coincidences.

One of the clearest methods of communication with God for me has been through meditation. I learned to meditate using a mantra during my early 20's. I use a very simple method of sitting or lying quietly and repeating a short phrase on the in breath and a short phrase on the out breath. The two can be the same as in repeating the mantra Om Namah Shivaya on both the in and out breaths as I was originally taught. At some point the practice changes from consciously repeating the mantra as a tool to avoid distracting thoughts, to hearing it internally without effort. At that point, thoughts are no longer a distraction. For the last few years, I have been simply saying/hearing "light" on in breath and "love" on the out breath; these words being two of the primary attributes of God.

I find meditation to be a way to quickly relax, to distract from pain or discomfort, to pleasantly pass time while unable to sleep, and most importantly, to put me in a quiet receptive state to hear the voice of God within or to connect to the cosmic heart. From there I frequently send positive intentions to others and ask that they be blessed. Prior to meditation, I set up the understanding and condition that anything I receive in my meditation is in keeping with the highest and best purpose of creation and to block out everything else. It is my way of protecting my line of communications with the Divine so it cannot be hacked into and manipulated.

In addition to this world being a school for learning about love, many souls also chose to have incarnations in this third dimensional reality because of the texture available here that could not be experienced from a more ethereal vantage point. It is like the difference between watching a movie about life versus actually being alive or the difference between reading about love and actually being in love. From what I understand, running through a field and feeling the wind and the sun is just not an experience you can have without a physical third dimensional body, which is simply not available in the ethereal realms.

One aspect of creation of which I am fully convinced is that we are actually light beings temporarily inhabiting physical bodies, but living in an illusion created by God that these temporary bodies are our real selves. To honor the creation and God, I am in agreement with being alive in this world and learning the lessons that are being taught in this Earthly school with grace and a loving heart. I act as if I had free will and choice, whether or not that is true. My prescription for living is to be true to my role in the illusion called life; to act with love and integrity; to accept the pleasures, pains, successes, and failures of life as they unfold; and to know that God showers me with love and abundance and is my constant companion.

        With love and light,
        JOSEPH ANTHONY

NOTES

These are my working understandings of terms from the channeling sessions.

Arcturian
: The Arcturians are thought to be a master healing race that live in the Belt of Orion.

Crystalline Body, Density and Dimension
: Both density (physicality) and dimension (consciousness) correspond to the chakras. Someone predominately vibrating at the solar plexus level, which is the third charka, would be at the third-dimensional level. A person predominately vibrating at the heart level, which is the fourth charka, would largely be living at the fourth-dimensional level. Most people on Earth are operating at the third-dimensional level most of the time, but there are many humans living at the fourth. Both have the same carbon-based physical bodies at the third level of density. The difference between them is largely one of consciousness and attunement to divinity. Beings existing at the astral level would be fourth density and those at the fifth density would have crystalline-based bodies, which are sometimes called light bodies. They would be at a fifth-dimensional or higher vibrational rate and level of consciousness.

Metatron
: Metatron is considered to be an Archangel by many, and Metatron's cube is a geometric pattern of connected circles and squares thought to have spiritual energy.

Transition, Ascension and Shift

These terms are used interchangeably and refer to an anticipated planet-wide shift or ascension from the earth's current third dimension of spirituality to a higher dimension of spirituality. That shift would bring numerous positive changes to humanity including a greater awareness of God, a truer understanding of reality, a sense of harmony with all life, and enhanced ability to create.

ACKNOWLEDGEMENTS

THIS BOOK COULD never have come into existence without involvement of so many souls, both human and in spirit form, that it would be hard to count them. I am truly grateful for this help. It was a high point of my life to be part of the process of creating this book. But I in no way can take credit for more than a small piece of it, mostly as a scribe and compiler.

Major credit for the creation of this book rests with Spirit. All of the information in the first part of the book came from Spirit through channelers (Sage, Johanna, Carylanne, and the Healing Light Group members) who are all deeply connected to spirit. As I mentioned previously, it was also Spirit that told me through three different channelers that I should bring this book forward. It was also Spirit, communicating through meditation and intuition, which provided guidance on what should be included and how it might be arranged.

My wife, Laura, and my good friend Albert are largely responsible for transforming the initial manuscript from a somewhat raw collection of transcribed recordings into a coherent book. They each made insightful suggestions on format and content as well as did critical proofreading. Albert also very ably shepherded the final manuscript through the publication process.

The Healing Light Group members generously allowed me to record their sessions and provided an environment that facilitated a connection and exploration of the metaphysical realms. They are my most valued colleagues, and this book would not have happened without their cooperation and support.

Finally, I am most grateful for my muse and four-legged companion Tucker. He stayed faithfully by my side during the many hours and days I spent working on the computer or listening to the recordings, never failing to interrupt me every hour or two with a ball or stuffed animal to remind me of the ongoing importance of play in a balanced life.

ABOUT THE AUTHOR

Joseph Anthony's spiritual unfolding began in his early twenties with a profound experience of cosmic unity in which he saw everything as a single divine, loving, conscious energy. Nothing was excluded; even the air was conscious and appeared as dancing pinpoints of light. He knew instantly that this was the true reality, and that what he had previously thought to be real was, as one of his later teachers said, only a "play of consciousness." The experience opened up an active channel to the higher realms for him that manifested as enhanced intuition and direct messages and guidance from higher beings.

Joseph's life experiences reveal the omnipresence of God, the nature of the soul, the work of Lightworkers, and the guidance available from ethereal spirits such as angels, dragons and departed masters. In 2012, he was guided along with three friends to set up a group of sixteen Lightworkers who worked together to send energy to problems throughout the world. To do this, they used crystals, healing meditation and the channeling of higher dimensional beings. Joseph also has experienced how life flows when attuned to a fourth dimensional consciousness.

As a young adult, Joseph's mystical revelation showed him that all is God and that his life's purpose would be to know, love and serve God. At age 25, Joseph was diagnosed with Stage III Hodgkin's Disease. After treatment, while working as a carpenter, he was divinely inspired to go back to school. He earned a doctorate in psychology and worked for 20 years in an academic cancer center as a behavioral medicine researcher. His life's work has been about learning to understand the nature of God at work in our world and, in a very personal way, in our lives.

Contact Information

Email: JosephAnthony@ListeningtoSpirit.net
URL: ListeningtoSpirit.net